THAI FOOD
MADE EASY

THAI FOOD
MADE EASY

TOM KIME

PHOTOGRAPHS BY LISA LINDER

MURDOCH BOOKS

SYDNEY · LONDON

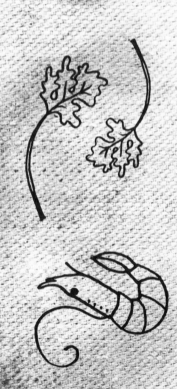

Contents

Thai Food ****

is electrifying and **invigorating** and makes the tongue tingle with excitement. You can remember the first time you tasted it. When you try the real stuff, you are soon hooked. You are literally craving more and more amazing flavours. Chilli is actually addictive and makes you feel **good** when you eat it, so maybe this is the reason why.

The myth of Thai cooking is that its exotic secrets are hard to master, out of reach for the every day cook. We instead settle for cheap takeaway, which seemed like a good idea at the time but is usually disappointing.

Cooking really good authentic Thai food is actually relatively simple. There is a bit of prep to do but the cooking process is not that hard. What is vital is getting a balance of taste. In Thailand this is called 'ROT CHART', where flavours are enhanced and defined. Rot — meaning 'taste' — and chart — meaning 'proper', 'unified', 'balanced' — is the ultimate goal of Thai cooking.

In Thai cooking there are four main groups of taste: hot, sweet, sour and salty. HOT includes pepper and spice, represented by fresh and dried chilli, whole and ground pepper, dried and fresh spices, ginger, garlic, galangal and turmeric. The chemical opposite of hot is SWEET, which comes from sugar, palm sugar, fruit or honey as well as toasted coconut or coconut cream. More complex sweet elements are prawns or seafood such as crab, slow roast pork or duck. Lime and lemon juice and rice vinegar are SOUR, as are the complex characteristics of tamarind, lemongrass and kaffir lime leaves. The SALT in Thai cooking comes from fish sauce, soy sauce, savoury toasted nuts, salted smoked fish and dried prawns.

All of these tastes must be in balance in every mouthful and in every dish. The key to mastering this balance of flavours is by tasting your food throughout the cooking process. This sounds simple, doesn't it? However, most cooks do not do it often enough. Take a piece of watermelon and eat it, then squeeze some lime and taste it again: this is much more exciting. Season again with salt and lime and taste — now things are beginning to hot up. Finally, sprinkle a little dried chilli or crushed black pepper on the watermelon. With salt and lime you have created extraordinary food that sparks a firework display on your tastebuds. This is Thai cooking. Once tried, there is no turning back.

TOP 12 STAR
Experiences
in Thailand

I. Take your elephant for a river bath in the northern jungle of Chiang Mai and sample some kai yang: Isaan-style chicken with lemongrass and black pepper.

2. Have an authentic massage in the Thai massage school at Wat Pho, the temple of the reclining buddha in Bangkok. Eat Thai fishcakes or banana fritters from one of the stalls outside the temple.

3. Sip a mai tai cocktail overlooking the beach in Phuket. Admire the view and enjoy some turmeric-grilled fish or a bowl of spice-fried squid.

4. Have a Singha beer at a Thai kickboxing competition. Get a real kick with a Thai beef stir-fry with chilli and onion relish.

5. Eat street food while being gracefully rowed around the historic floating markets of Amphawa. Why not try a hot and sour green papaya salad to really feel at home?

6. Eat a jungle curry, looking out over the jungle. Originating from northern Thailand, these curries are very fiery and have no coconut cream. They were historically made with wild boar. If you can't stand the heat and you want something a bit less hot, then how about a red curry with caramelised chicken?

7. Buy a Chanel bag or a Rolex for a few dollars in a night market while enjoying some banana and coconut pancakes or sweet and crispy pork spare ribs.

8. Take a slow ride in a cyclo to experience the crazy atmosphere in Bangkok. Why not eat some hakka-style fried pork noodles?

9. Find your own ideal beach. Don't bother going with all the other tourists to visit Maya Bay, the film set from *The Beach*. Instead, find your own piece of paradise. Or simply drink a pineapple mint ginger crush and close your eyes and dream.

10. Take part in a hands-on Thai cooking class in a royal palace and learn how to make spicy ocean broth with herbed fishcakes.

11. Lay in an island hammock sipping a freshly picked young coconut. Why not try the set coconut cream — simple and exotic — just like a Thai island hammock.

12. Pick your own spices in a pepper plantation while cycling around the picturesque countryside, then enjoy some crispy fried whitebait with Thai spices or fragrant chicken wings with galangal.

NIGHT MARKET
Banana & coconut pancakes

CHIANG MAI
Kai yang (Isaan-style chicken with lemongrass & black pepper)

NORTHERN JUNGLE
Jungle curry

PEPPER PLANTATION
Crispy fried whitebait with Thai spices

ROYAL PALACE BANGKOK
Spicy ocean broth with herbed fishcakes

BANGKOK

TEMPLE OF THE RECLINING BUDDHA
Thai fishcakes

FLOATING MARKETS OF AMPHAWA
Hot and sour green papaya salad

BANGKOK CYCLO
Hakka-style fried pork noodles

ISLAND LIFE
Set coconut cream

PHUKET
Mai tai cocktail & spice-fried squid

BEACH PARADISE
Pineapple mint ginger crush

Ingredients
for Thai cooking

Fresh ingredients, nuts & seeds

LEMONGRASS

Lemongrass imparts all the citrus flavours of lemon and lime but without the acidity and bitterness. When using, remove all the tough outer leaves. Buy fresh stems that are bulbous at the bottom and near white in colour. Use a sharp knife to finely slice the stems into thin slivers. Lemongrass can be eaten raw in salads, used as a garnish or puréed and cooked in curry pastes. You can also cut it into thin slices, freeze it and use it directly from the freezer.

GINGER

Ginger has extraordinary culinary and medicinal value. When buying, make sure you choose plump young pieces. The skin and peelings can be crushed and puréed for soups and curry pastes. The flesh can be shredded and eaten raw in salads or as a garnish.

CORIANDER ROOTS

These sound exotic but are really as simple as they sound: the roots at the bottom of a bunch of coriander. If you are growing your own coriander, instead of cutting the stems, pull the whole thing out like a bunch of carrots. The roots provide an intense flavour when used in pastes, marinades and dressings. If the roots are not available, use the lower part of the stems instead and finely chop them. They can be bought in bags in good Asian grocery stores. The roots can be finely chopped or pounded and eaten raw or cooked.

THAI BASIL

Thai basil has shiny dark green leaves that are more spear-shaped than Western basil and often have a purple tinge. Thai basil has a strong lemony star anise–aniseed taste, which is very distinctive. Try to find it fresh where possible as dried or frozen is not as good. It is available from Asian stores, but use some fragrant Western basil if you can't find any.

KAFFIR LIME LEAVES

These are the dark shiny leaves from the kaffir lime tree. They have the most amazing heady aroma when broken or torn and impart an extraordinary perfume and fragrance. You can buy them dried; however, if you freeze them from fresh, they keep their colour and flavour. If not available, use fresh lime zest instead as it provides all the citrus aroma and taste without any of the acidity. To shred kaffir lime leaves, trim the raised stem on the underside of the leaf, tightly roll the leaves into a cigar shape and cut across in very thin slices to produce a fine shred.

CHILLI

The use of chilli is important in Thai cooking as it provides the heat to balance the other flavours. Chillies vary in strength so always taste a little before you add any to your dish. It is much easier to increase the heat than try to take it away from your food. The small bird's eye chillies are the hottest. Dry chilli is also much hotter than fresh chilli. A number of the recipes call for seeded and finely chopped long red chillies: this is a way of you having a bit more control of the heat content. With a complete balance of taste the opposite of peppery hot is sweet. If your dish is too hot then temper it with something sweet or neutral such as coconut cream, palm sugar or fruit.

GARLIC

Garlic is used in a lot of Thai cooking, although it is possible to make this cuisine without it, if there is an allergy; simply use more ginger, coriander root and chilli. When garlic is used in a dressing or paste it will be eaten raw. For this reason a mortar and pestle is essential for the Thai cook. The garlic cloves can be crushed with a little salt so they are not big chunks in a raw dressing. Raw garlic is peppery hot, but when it is cooked it becomes sweet and rich tasting.

BLANCHED SKINLESS PEANUTS

Toasted peanuts are used in many different Thai dishes. You can buy unsalted peanuts either with or without the skin from Asian grocery stores. Dry-roast peanuts over medium heat in a frying pan or in a moderate oven until they are golden brown. Do not make them too dark as they will be bitter. Leave to cool and then crush or chop. Always check if anyone has a peanut allergy before serving.

CASHEWS

Buy raw unsalted cashews. Dry-roast until golden brown. If you are preparing Thai food for someone who has a nut allergy you can use toasted rice to form the nutty texture in the dish (see page 17) instead.

SESAME SEEDS

Sesame seeds provide a much needed texture to Thai dishes. Dry-fry sesame seeds over medium heat or in the oven until golden brown and crunchy.

Spices

TURMERIC

Turmeric is the root of a plant related to ginger and can be used fresh in many dishes; however, fresh turmeric is not readily available so dried ground turmeric is used in all of the recipes in this book. Turmeric is peppery hot with an aromatic and slightly earthy taste. The bright yellow colour is a very strong dye that has been used for thousands of years for this very purpose. Make sure when you are using it in the kitchen that you only add it to food when it is cooking in a stainless steel pan or bowl. If turmeric powder comes into contact with anything plastic, such as a food processor bowl or a spatula, it will dye it a deep yellow–orange colour. A little dried turmeric goes a long way but it is essential for curry pastes. The colour is warm and welcoming.

CINNAMON

Cinnamon is a warm and generous spice with a flavour that evokes memories of Christmas. Available as sticks or ground, it is a delicious addition to your food. Cinnamon is often used in desserts and that is where it is most familiar (try the spice-roast pears or the banana pancakes); however, it is also used in the Geng gari curry (see page 226) and Spiced bavette steak (see page 94). Ground cinnamon responds really well and becomes fragrant and aromatic when it is dry-roasted or comes into contact with direct heat. Grind your own spices in a small electric spice or coffee grinder or using a mortar and pestle.

CUMIN SEEDS

Cumin seeds are at their best and most delicious when they are dry-roasted until aromatic and then freshly ground. This is a spice that is predominantly associated with Indian cooking; however, it is often used in Thai cooking in particular curry pastes such as geng gari and massaman pastes (see pages 226 and 228). Roasted cumin provides a delicious three-dimensional depth of flavour when used in roast duck curry or spice fried squid or grilled meat.

CORIANDER SEEDS

Coriander seeds could not taste more different from fresh coriander or coriander roots, all of which are used frequently in the Thai kitchen. Always use whole seeds that you then crush or grind yourself, as you will get a much cleaner and more aromatic taste. Ground spices are convenient but they are often dusty and stale and you do not know how long ago they were ground. When you grind your own spices you get lots of flavour and a little texture to the grind, which is really important. Like cumin, coriander seeds work well when they are lightly roasted until fragrant, then crushed using a mortar and pestle or ground in an electric grinder.

STAR ANISE

This is a truly amazing spice that has an extraordinary taste. The intense perfume of aniseed is very evocative when you first smell it in a Thai street food market or with some slow roast pork belly. Simply break the hard spices into a few pieces so that you release the oils and aromatic qualities when it is cooking. You can also grind the spices in a spice grinder for use in spice blends. Star anise is delicious with roasted caramelised meat, such as pork or beef.

PEPPER

Dried black and white pepper are both frequently used whole, or finely and coarsely ground. Fresh green peppercorns still on the vine are also used and added to curries and soups to provide a bite. Much of Thai cuisine contains chillies, either fresh or dried; however, it was only after the Portuguese had travelled to South America in the 16th century that chillies were introduced to southern Asia and South–East Asia, including Thailand. Previous to this, black and white pepper was used to create heat, along with ingredients such as ginger and garlic.

FIVE-SPICE

There are many combinations of spice mixes throughout Thailand and South–East Asia. They are at the best and most fragrant when ground to order from whole spices, then blended. Five-spice powder has both medicinal and culinary importance and is used to season meats and poultry in China, Vietnam and Thailand. It frequently contains fennel seeds and star anise, cinnamon, cloves and sichuan pepper, and it has a very distinctive aroma. Try making your own blend and you will never look back.

SEN MEE NOODLES

SEN LEK NOODLES

STICKY RICE

JASMINE RICE

BASMATI RICE

SEN YAI NOODLES

Pantry/larder

SPRING ROLL WRAPPERS

This is paper-thin pastry that is bought prerolled in packets and is available from Asian grocery stores and good supermarkets. Keep the packet sealed so that pastry layers do not dry out.

RICE NOODLES

There are numerous widths of rice noodles that are bought dried. They need to be soaked in warm water for 20 minutes before using.

SEN MEE are very fine and wiry when dried and are also called rice vermicelli. They are used in spring rolls, soups, stir-fries and salads.

SEN YAI are broad in width (about 2–3 cm wide) and are also called rice river noodles and rice sticks. When they are bought fresh they can be quite sticky and need to be separated. Good for a stir-fry such as Pad thai (see page 176) where there is lots of sauce.

SEN LEK are a thinner rice noodle (about 1 cm in width). They are commonly sold dried and are probably the most widely available. Soak before cooking and they will only take a couple of minutes to cook.

BA MEE noodles are made with egg and rice flour so they are a mid-yellow colour and similar to Italian spaghetti. These are often used for stir-fries and soups.

WUN SEN are very fine — almost translucent — in colour and are made with soya flour. They are called cellophane or glass noodles. They will not need a lot of cooking and are great for salads and cold noodle dishes with prawns and seafood.

THAI STICKY OR GLUTINOUS RICE

This is a particular variety of short-grain rice. It needs to be soaked in cold running water before it is steamed and is often used for desserts.

THAI JASMINE OR FRAGRANT RICE

This is a longer-grain rice that is used to accompany curries and is essentially served at every meal in Thai cooking. If you have rice even with a simple sauce it is considered a meal. This is still quite a starchy rice so it does need to be soaked before it is cooked, and can be cooked in a rice cooker.

BASMATI RICE

Basmati rice is a long-grain Indian rice: its name means 'fragrant'. This type of grain is much less starchy than Thai short-grain rices. It is perfect for making a pilaf and will accompany any Thai curry if you do not have any Thai jasmine or sticky rice to hand.

* how to *
TOAST & GRIND RICE

* *Preheat the oven to 170°C.*

* *Scatter 80–100 g uncooked jasmine or Thai rice on a baking tray. Bake for about 6–8 minutes, until the rice is evenly golden and fragrant. Check regularly while cooking to avoid scorching.*

* *When the rice is cool, grind using a mortar and pestle or an electric spice grinder until it resembles a fine grain that is similar to sesame seeds. Alternatively, you can use toasted sesame seeds instead.*

* *You can keep the toasted and ground rice in an airtight container for about 10 days and use it for other recipes.*

Liquids

COCONUT MILK & CREAM

This is available in tins from supermarkets and Asian grocery stores. There are lots of varieties, but I would always opt for one that has a Thai label. The liquid inside the tin is made up of thinner coconut milk and thicker coconut cream. It can be stirred and used together or some recipes will call for the two parts to be used at separate points during cooking.

SOY SAUCE

There are two main types of soy sauce. Light soy sauce is light coloured, almost translucent, and is the more salty of the two. It is used to provide the much needed salty element in Thai cuisine. Dark soy sauce is thicker and stronger tasting and is made richer with the addition of a little molasses. There is also a sweet soy sauce often called ABC sauce or kecap manis, which is thicker and richer and sweeter still. A little of this goes a long way.

BLENDED SESAME OIL

This is mid-brown in colour and intensely nutty in flavour. Use it sparingly as it has quite a noticeable flavour. This is another salty, savoury, smoky element that adds complexity to a dish and is often used in dressings.

FISH SAUCE

This is the fundamental salty and savoury flavouring in Thai and South–East Asian cuisine. In Thailand it is called nam pla and in Vietnam it is called nuoc mam. It is made from salting and fermenting small fish, with fish sauce being the run-off liquid. It can vary in saltiness: the lighter and more golden whisky-coloured it is the better. If it is very dark then it is older and could be bitter. Fish sauce on its own is not a pleasant experience; however, when combined with lime juice there is a great balance of taste. If you have added too much fish sauce, then add some more lime juice to temper the saltiness.

PRAWN PASTE

This dark purple paste, also known as gapi shrimp paste, has a very pungent smell when it is raw (you would be forgiven for thinking that there must be some mistake: how could you possibly add this to your food?) When roasted or grilled it loses all its pungency and provides

OYSTER SAUCE

COCONUT MILK

SESAME OIL

RICE VINEGAR

FISH SAUCE

a rich savoury taste to a dish. Use sparingly and keep sealed in an airtight container.

TAMARIND PULP

Tamarind is the pulp from the pods of the tamarind tree. It is dark and sticky, like a date, and has an extraordinary taste that is sweet and yet makes your mouth pucker with sourness. It is high in vitamin C and provides a depth of intensely sour flavour to a dish, especially curries. Tamarind pulp is available in jars and tubs in Asian grocery stores. It is also available as a compressed block of sticky meat. To use this, soak a tablespoon-sized nugget in warm water. Knead the tamarind until it has dissolved and

the water is a deep brown colour. This is tamarind water or tamarind liquid. Avoid buying tamarind concentrate as it is too dark and sour and makes your food a very dark colour.

RICE VINEGAR

This is a clear potent vinegar that is used in many Thai dips and sauces. It is best to buy this as it is authentic; however, any plain white wine vinegar could be used instead.

OYSTER SAUCE

This is a condiment originally made from simmering oysters until they were thick and caramelised.

The modern version is made by simmering salt, sugar and cornflour with oyster essence. The result is a highly flavoured sauce that is full of umami savoury flavourings. It is sweet, salty and great with stir-fried greens.

PALM SUGAR

This is made from the cooked sap of the coconut palm. It is sold in blocks, nuggets or compressed cakes. Palm sugar can vary in colour and texture: some are more like fudge while others are dark and very hard. The best is a golden brown and has a toffee nutty aroma and taste. If it's not available, you can use soft brown sugar but it will not be quite the same.

PRAWN PASTE

TAMARIND PULP

PALM SUGAR

SOY SAUCE

15
MUST-HAVE
HERBS &
SPICES

·1·
LEMONGRASS

Spiced prawn cakes on lemongrass sticks, p.30

Grilled prawn & basil salad, p.62

Isaan-style grilled chicken with black pepper & lemongrass, p.84

Roast duck soup with lime, chilli & basil, p.170

Sesame-seared tuna with lemongrass & ginger, p.124

·2·
GINGER

Braised mushrooms with ginger & chilli, p.192

Grilled fish with chilli, garlic & ginger, p.148

Tea-smoked trout with toasted coconut & ginger, p.140

Hot & sour soup with roasted shallots, chicken & Thai basil, p.168

Thai beef skewers with red chilli vinegar, p.88

·3·
BLACK & WHITE PEPPERCORNS

Sesame chicken salad with white pepper, p.64

Siamese chicken with ginger, coriander, garlic & white pepper, p.98

Stir-fried spinach with garlic & black pepper, p.194

Watermelon with lime, salt & black pepper, 210

Red curry paste, p.223

·4·
FIVE-SPICE

Thai beef skewers with red chilli vinegar, p.88

Crispy chicken spring rolls with chilli & ginger, p.28

Pork & pickled cucumber salad, p.72

Stir-fried cod with sugar snap peas, ginger & five-spice, p.134

·5·
THAI BASIL

Grilled prawn & basil salad, p.62

Stir-fried mussels & clams with chilli jam, p.146

Hot & sour soup with roasted shallots, chicken & basil, p.168

Red curry with chicken, p.156

Roast duck soup with lime, chilli & basil, p.170

·6·
CORIANDER SEEDS

Salt & spice-roast pork belly, p.100

Siamese chicken with ginger, coriander, garlic & white pepper, p.98

Aromatic smoked fish, p.138

Salt & pepper mix, p.246

Geng gari spiced curry with roast chicken, p.166

·7·
CHILLI

Chilli tamarind caramel, p.235

Hot & sour green mango salad, p.60

Thai green curry with prawns, p.154

Chicken & coconut milk soup, p.172

Glass noodle & pork spring rolls, p.24

Crab & lime salad with coriander & chilli, p.74

·8·
CORIANDER ROOTS

Fried crab cakes with coriander, p.50

Thai beef skewers with red chilli vinegar, p.88

Creamy pumpkin soup, p.158

Braised chicken with rice, turmeric & spices, p.186

Hot & sour orange curry paste, p.227

·9·
STAR ANISE

Salt & spice-roast pork belly, p.100

Aromatic smoked fish salad, p.70

Pineapple with caramelised chilli caramel, p.208

Sweet & crispy pork spare ribs, p.110

Roasted fruits with Thai aromatic spices, p.218

·10·
CARDAMOM

Spiced banana fritters, p.200

Fragrant chicken wings with galangal, p.90

Salt & spice-roast pork belly, p.100

Spice marinade for duck & chicken, p.230

Set coconut cream, p.158

·11·
KAFFIR LIME LEAVES

Thai fishcakes with cucumber pickle, p.48

Cured prawns with ginger & kaffir lime leaves, p.36

Coconut fish curry, p.152

Spicy beef noodles with shredded kaffir lime leaves, p.180

Chicken & coconut milk soup, p.172

·12·
GARLIC

Fried crab cakes with coriander , p.50

Tamarind fried beef with peanuts, p.86

Green chilli nahm jim, p.237

Sweet chilli sauce, p.238

Marinated prawn satay, p.144

Grilled squid with garlic & black pepper, p.40

·13·
TURMERIC

Chicken satay with turmeric & ginger, p.32

Turmeric grilled fish, p.130

Barbecued pork & herb salad, p.92

Coconut fish curry, p.152

Southern Thai barbecued chicken, p.44

Caramelised chilli roast chicken, p.112

·14·
CINNAMON

Banana & coconut pancakes, p.214

Fragrant chicken wings with galangal p.90

Hot & sour grilled beef salad, p.56

Aromatic smoked fish, p.138

Toasted coconut ice-cream topping, p.212

·15·
CUMIN SEEDS

Salt & pepper mix, p.246

Massaman curry paste with toasted peanuts, p.228

Siamese chicken with ginger, coriander, garlic & white pepper, p.98

Geng gari curry with roast chicken, p.166

Snacks & finger food

chapter 1

Glass noodle & pork spring rolls

Street food is enjoyed by everyone across Thailand. There are hundreds of variations of spring rolls using different filling ingredients. This is one of my favourites.

serves 6
● ● ● ● ●
(makes 18)

preparation
20 minutes

soaking
10 minutes

cooking
5 minutes per batch

fresh
500 g lean pork mince

2 garlic cloves, finely chopped

2 red chillies, seeded and finely chopped

3 coriander sprigs, leaves picked and coarsely chopped

Green chilli nahm jim (see page 237), to serve

spices
1 tablespoon freshly ground black pepper

pantry/larder
200 g thin glass noodles or rice noodles

1 tablespoon fish sauce

½ teaspoon salt

1 teaspoon soft brown sugar

200 ml vegetable oil

18 spring roll wrappers (3 per person)

1. Soak the noodles in a bowl of cold water for 10 minutes to soften. Drain, then put the noodles in a saucepan of lightly salted boiling water and cook for about 4 minutes until al dente. Strain, then run under cold water to refresh them. Use a pair of scissors to cut the noodles into 2 cm lengths.

2. Put the pork mince in a large bowl and add the chopped noodles, fish sauce, salt, sugar and black pepper. Mix together, then add the garlic, chillies and coriander and mix again.

3. Heat a small amount of oil in a frying pan over medium heat. Fry a small ball of meat mixture for a few minutes until cooked. Taste the cooked meat to check the balance of flavours and adjust if needed, remembering that the dipping sauce will be salty, hot and sour, too.

4. Use the spring roll wrappers and prepared filling to roll the springs rolls following the instructions on pages 26–27.

5. Prepare the oil as instructed on page 27 and fry the spring rolls in small batches for about 4 minutes, moving the spring rolls around in the pan and turning them so they become golden brown all over.

6. Use a slotted spoon to remove the rolls and place them on paper towel to absorb any excess oil. Allow the oil to reheat for a minute before cooking the next batch. Serve with Green chilli nahm jim for dipping.

how to make
SPRING ROLLS

makes: 18 * preparation: 10 minutes * cooking: 5 minutes per batch

 equipment: small bowl of water, pastry brush, clean tea towel, lightly oiled tray or plate, wok, vegetable oil for deep-frying

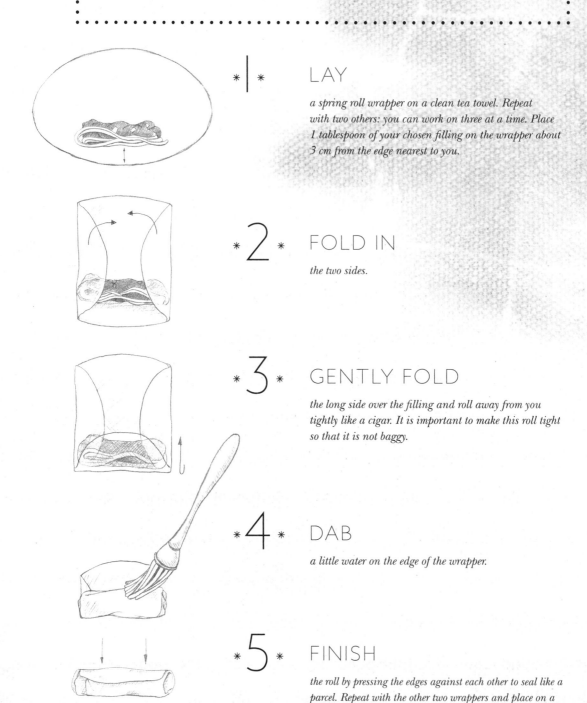

| LAY

a spring roll wrapper on a clean tea towel. Repeat with two others: you can work on three at a time. Place 1 tablespoon of your chosen filling on the wrapper about 3 cm from the edge nearest to you.

2 FOLD IN

the two sides.

3 GENTLY FOLD

the long side over the filling and roll away from you tightly like a cigar. It is important to make this roll tight so that it is not baggy.

4 DAB

a little water on the edge of the wrapper.

5 FINISH

the roll by pressing the edges against each other to seal like a parcel. Repeat with the other two wrappers and place on a lightly oiled plate.

There are hundreds of variations for the fillings and dipping sauces for Thai spring rolls. You can easily use some leftovers to make a delicious snack — a few prawns or some cooked chicken or pork will go a long way when mixed with herbs and other aromatic ingredients to make the filling.

* 6 *

PLACE

a wok or a high-sided heavy-based pan over medium heat. Heat for a couple of minutes before filling the wok one-third full of vegetable oil ready for deep-frying (the oil can be re-used when cool). If the oil is hot enough to fry, drop a small piece of bread into the oil. It should sizzle and give off bubbles straight away. If it doesn't, remove the bread and try again. When the oil is hot enough, reduce the heat slightly to keep a constant temperature.

FRY

the spring rolls in small batches so that the oil remains hot. Move the spring rolls with a slotted spoon around the wok for about 4 minutes, turning them so they become golden brown all over. Use a slotted spoon to lift the cooked spring rolls out of the oil and place on paper towel to absorb any excess oil. Allow the oil to reheat for a minute before cooking the next batch. Serve with dipping sauce and fresh herbs.

* 7 *

Good spring rolls are delicate in size and shape: 3 cm wide and 6–8 cm long. Make sure that they are tight and firm when rolling and don't make them too big.

Put the dipping sauce and the separate herbs in the centre of the table. Take a hot spring roll, wrap a couple of leaves around it, dip into the sauce and enjoy.

Crispy chicken spring rolls
with chilli & ginger

serves 4

● ● ● ●

(makes 12)

preparation

50 minutes

cooking

15 minutes per batch

Simply wrap the fried spring rolls in coriander leaves and dip in the sauce to enjoy.

fresh

2 garlic cloves, finely chopped

1 red chilli, finely chopped

4 cm piece of ginger, peeled and grated

200 g oyster mushrooms, finely chopped

50 g onion, finely chopped

250 g chicken mince

4 spring onions, finely chopped

2 eggs

a handful of coriander, leaves picked and coarsely chopped (reserve some whole leaves to serve)

Sweet chilli sauce (see page 238) or Hot and sour red chilli dressing (see page 234), to serve

spices

freshly ground black pepper

1 teaspoon five-spice powder

pantry/larder

¼ teaspoon salt

2 tablespoons fish sauce

200 ml vegetable oil

12 spring roll wrappers (3 per person)

1. Heat a heavy-based pan over high heat. Add a little oil, then add the garlic, chilli and ginger. Turn the heat down to medium and fry for 2 minutes until fragrant and aromatic. Add the mushrooms and the onion, turn up the heat and fry quickly until they are browned with a nutty aroma. Season with the salt and black pepper.

2. Mix the chicken, spring onions, eggs, coriander, five-spice powder and fish sauce in a large bowl and add the fried mixture. Heat a tiny bit of oil in a frying pan over medium heat and fry a small piece of the mixture for a minute or two until cooked. Taste it and adjust the seasoning if needed, remembering that the dipping sauce will be hot, salty and sour.

3. Use the spring roll wrappers and prepared filling to roll the springs rolls following the instructions on pages 26–27.

4. Prepare the oil as instructed on page 27 and fry the spring rolls in small batches for about 5 minutes, moving the spring rolls around in the pan and turning them so they become golden brown all over. Use a slotted spoon to remove the rolls and place on paper towel to absorb any excess oil. Allow the oil to reheat for a minute before cooking the next batch. To eat, wrap a few coriander leaves around the spring rolls, before dipping in your chosen dipping sauce.

Chao tom
spiced prawn cakes on lemongrass sticks

serves 6
• • • • •
(makes 24)

preparation
10 minutes

cooking
4 minutes

Chao tom is a spiced prawn paté, which can be grilled, fried or wrapped in banana leaves and steamed. The lemongrass sticks infuse the prawn paté with a lovely aromatic flavour.

fresh

12 lemongrass stems

1 kg large raw tiger prawns, peeled and deveined

1 eggwhite

2 garlic cloves, finely chopped

3 cm piece of ginger, peeled and finely chopped

2 red chillies, seeded and finely chopped

a handful of coriander, leaves picked and coarsely chopped

juice of 1 lime

Green chilli nahm jim (see page 237), to serve

spices

freshly ground black pepper

pantry/larder

1 tablespoon fish sauce

1 tablespoon rice flour

salt

1. Trim the root end of the lemongrass, but leave the core which will hold the stem together. Cut the stems to about 10–12 cm in length. Remove the tough outer leaves and cut the stems in half through the core so that you have 24 sticks held in place by the core.

2. Place all of the ingredients except the lemongrass in a food processor or blender, add some salt and black pepper and blend into a paste. Do not overblend or the mixture will become tough. Fry a small piece of the mixture so that you can taste and adjust the seasoning accordingly.

3. Preheat a griddle pan or barbecue on high heat. Roll the mixture into balls and press a lemongrass stick into each one. Mould the paté around the stem like a lollipop. Grill the prawn cakes on the hot griddle or barbecue for about 2 minutes on each side until golden brown on both sides and the meat is firm. Serve with a Thai dipping sauce, such as Green chilli nahm jim.

This recipe is traditionally made using sugar cane sticks, but as they are quite hard to find I have used lemongrass here, which imparts its unique perfume right into the centre of the prawn cakes.

CHEF'S TIP

Chicken satay
with turmeric & ginger

Satay essentially means 'stick' and there are scores of varieties of this recipe across Thailand. These ones are great with the flavours of lemongrass and turmeric.

serves 4-6

●●●–●●●●●

preparation
10 minutes

marinating
1 hour

cooking
18 minutes

fresh

2 onions, chopped

5 cm piece of ginger, peeled and finely grated

2 lemongrass stems, tough outer leaves removed and stems finely chopped

2 garlic cloves, finely chopped

2 medium-hot red chillies, seeded and finely chopped

juice of 1 lime

1 kg chicken thigh fillets, cut into 3 cm cubes

Peanut dipping sauce (see page 242), to serve

spices

½ teaspoon freshly ground black pepper

2 teaspoons ground turmeric

pantry/larder

2 tablespoons fish sauce

1 tablespoon tamarind pulp

½ teaspoon salt

bamboo skewers soaked in cold water for 30 minutes

1. Put the onions, ginger, lemongrass, garlic and chillies in a food processor or blender and blend until smooth. Add the lime juice, fish sauce, tamarind pulp, salt and black pepper and blend again.

2. Tip the puréed ingredients into a heavy-based pan, add the turmeric and mix it through. Simmer gently over medium–high heat for about 10 minutes until the onions are cooked. Leave the mixture to cool.

3. Pour the fried mixture over the chicken and thoroughly mix together so that the chicken is completely coated. Leave to marinate in the refrigerator for at least 1 hour.

4. Thread the chicken onto the soaked skewers, allowing 3 pieces of chicken per skewer.

5. Preheat the grill or barbecue to high heat and grill the chicken for 4 minutes on each side until cooked through and browned. To check that it is cooked, take one piece and cut it open: the meat should be white inside and not pink. Serve with Peanut dipping sauce.

Tod man khao pad
curried sweetcorn fritters

These crispy fritters are great when made with really sweet and crunchy fresh corn kernels. The curry paste added to the batter makes them a perfect snack because they stimulate all the tastebuds.

serves 4-6
●●●●—●●●●●

preparation
10 minutes

cooking
4–6 minutes per batch

fresh

4 corncobs

2 tablespoons Red or Green curry paste (see pages 223 and 224)

2 large eggs

4 spring onions, finely chopped

a handful of coriander, leaves picked and coarsely chopped

lime wedges or a dipping sauce made from lime juice or rice vinegar, to serve

spices

freshly ground black pepper

pantry/larder

6 tablespoons rice flour

1 tablespoon fish sauce

1 tablespoon light soy sauce

¼ teaspoon salt

vegetable oil, for shallow-frying

1. Use a sharp knife to cut the kernels from the corncob, but don't cut too much of the lower end of the husk, nearest the core of the cob.

2. Put the rice flour, curry paste, eggs, fish sauce, soy sauce, salt and pepper in a large mixing bowl. Mix together, then add the corn kernels, spring onions and coriander. If the batter is a little dry then also add 2 tablespoons of water.

3. Heat enough oil for shallow-frying in a large heavy-based saucepan over medium–high heat (see page 27 to test if the oil is hot enough). Drop a tablespoon of the batter into the hot oil and use the back of the spoon to flatten the mixture to form a rough patty or cake. Add a few more tablespoons of mixture to the oil and cook for 2–3 minutes on each side until golden brown and fragrant. Cook a few at a time in batches so that the oil does not drop in temperature.

4. Place the cooked fritters on paper towel to soak up any excess oil. Serve hot or at room temperature with lime wedges or a sour dipping sauce made with lime juice or rice vinegar.

Kung sang wa
cured prawns with ginger & kaffir lime leaves

serves 4
••••

preparation
10 minutes

cooking
4 minutes

This deliciously refreshing salad is perfect served as a party appetiser and is so quick to make.

fresh

12 large raw prawns, shells on

2 tablespoons lime juice

2 tablespoons orange juice

5 kaffir lime leaves, shredded

2 lemongrass stems, tough outer leaves removed and stems sliced

3 spring onions, finely chopped

4 cm piece of ginger, peeled and finely grated

2 medium-hot red chillies, seeded and finely chopped

4 mint sprigs, leaves picked

4 coriander sprigs, leaves picked

pantry/larder

2 tablespoons fish sauce

½ teaspoon caster sugar

1. Preheat a barbecue or griddle pan to high heat. Grill the prawns for 2 minutes on each side. Once cooked, peel and devein the prawns, then coarsely chop the meat and set aside.

2. Mix the citrus juices with the fish sauce and sugar in a bowl and stir to dissolve. Add the prawn meat and shredded kaffir lime leaves to the bowl and leave to cure for 3 minutes.

3. Add the remaining ingredients to the mixture, leaving the herbs until last. Taste to check the balance of flavours and adjust the seasoning to suit your taste.

CHEF'S TIP You could use other grilled shellfish such as crayfish, lobster or crab, which will also provide the sweet richness needed in this dish.

Tamarind fried prawns

The prawns are sweet and juicy, the tamarind is sour, the soy sauce is caramelised and salty and the chilli and black pepper is hot. You could also use this marinade for fish, other shellfish or chicken or pork.

serves 4-6

• • • – • • • • • •

preparation
5 minutes

marinating
30 minutes

cooking
4 minutes

fresh

600 g raw prawns, peeled and deveined, tails intact

a few coriander leaves, to garnish

spices

1 teaspoon freshly ground black pepper

¼ teaspoon crushed dried chilli

pantry/larder

2 tablespoons tamarind pulp

1 tablespoon light soy sauce

½ teaspoon soft brown sugar

a pinch of salt

2 tablespoons vegetable oil, for cooking

1. Mix all of the ingredients, except the prawns, salt and oil, together in a bowl. Add the prawns, cover and leave in the refrigerator for 30 minutes, turning 2–3 times during the marinating time.

2. Season the prawns with the salt. Heat the vegetable oil in a frying pan over medium–high heat and fry the prawns for about 2 minutes on each side until they are dark brown. Garnish with fresh coriander leaves and serve as a starter with some cucumber slices or as part of a larger meal with salads and roasted meats.

Don't add the salt to the marinade, or the prawns will leach out their liquid and juice, making them dried out and over-salty.

Grilled squid
with garlic & pepper

serves 4
••••

preparation
10 minutes

cooking
3 minutes

Dishes like this are found all around the coast of Thailand and South–East Asia. There are as many variations as there are little hawker stalls and portable grills selling them on the streets. Serve this as an aperitif or canapé or at the start of a barbecue.

fresh

2 garlic cloves, finely chopped

3 small green chillies, seeded and finely chopped

4 cm piece of ginger, peeled and finely grated

juice of 1 lemon

3 large squid (bodies about 15–23 cm long), cleaned, body and tentacles removed, and scored (see page 116 or ask your fishmonger to do this)

spices

½ teaspoon ground white pepper

pantry/larder

2 tablespoons fish sauce

1 teaspoon grated palm sugar (or coconut sugar or soft brown sugar)

salt

vegetable oil, for brushing

1. Preheat the barbecue or grill to high heat.

2. For the dipping sauce, mix the garlic, chillies, ginger, lemon juice and fish sauce together in a bowl. Stir in the palm sugar.

3. Pat the squid dry with paper towel and season with salt and the white pepper.

4. Brush the hot barbecue or grill with a little oil. Grill the squid on the unscored side first for 90 seconds. Turn the squid over with a pair of tongs and cook on the scored side for a further 60 seconds. Serve the grilled squid with the green chilli and garlic dipping sauce.

Miang of prawns

serves 4
● ● ● ●

preparation
10 minutes

cooking
7 minutes

This little dish has all the characteristics of authentic Thai cuisine. It is absolutely delicious and quite complex, which is why it works well as a small bite-sized taste explosion.

fresh

5 cm piece of ginger, peeled: 2 cm piece finely grated and the rest finely chopped

4 tablespoons toasted coconut

2 red chillies, seeded and finely chopped

1 lime, ½ juiced and the rest peeled and finely chopped

200 g cooked prawns, peeled, deveined and chopped if large

4 small shallots, finely diced

2 tablespoons blanched peanuts (dry-roasted until golden brown and coarsely ground using a mortar and pestle)

1 lemongrass stem, tough outer leaves removed and stems finely chopped

8 small iceberg lettuce leaves, to serve

pantry/larder

1 teaspoon prawn paste (see page 18)

2 tablespoons fish sauce

1 tablespoon palm sugar

1. Heat a frying pan over high heat. Once hot, add the finely grated ginger and prawn paste to the pan. Dry-fry, stirring, for 3 minutes or until the mixture is aromatic and golden.

2. Transfer the cooked mixture to a mortar and pestle and add half the roasted coconut and the chillies. Pound until smooth.

3. Return the mixture to the pan and add the fish sauce, palm sugar and 125 ml of water. Simmer for 7 minutes to reduce the sauce by half, then add the lime juice. Taste to check the balance of flavours: the sauce should be sweet, sour and salty with the heat coming from the fresh chilli.

4. Mix the prawns with the finely chopped lime, finely chopped ginger, 80 ml of the dressing, the remaining coconut and the remaining ingredients in a bowl. Serve on top of small iceberg lettuce leaves.

Southern Thai barbecued chicken

serves 4
• • • •

preparation
5 minutes

cooking
10 minutes

There will be a great balance of hot, sweet, salt and sour in these little chicken strips. They are deliciously spicy and will have your friends queuing up for more.

fresh

2 garlic cloves, finely chopped

1 small onion, chopped

300 g skinless chicken breast, cut into 5 mm slices

juice of 1 lime

4 coriander sprigs, to garnish

spices

1 teaspoon medium–hot curry powder

1 teaspoon ground coriander

½ teaspoon ground ginger

½ teaspoon ground turmeric

pantry/larder

2 tablespoons vegetable oil

4 tablespoons coconut cream

2 tablespoons fish sauce

1 teaspoon honey

1. Heat the vegetable oil in a wok or frying pan over medium–high heat and fry the garlic until golden brown. Add the onion, reduce the heat and stir-fry quickly for 3 minutes until the onion is softened.

2. Add the dried spices and cook for 1 minute until the spices are fragrant and aromatic. Add the coconut cream, fish sauce and honey and simmer for 2 minutes. Remove from the heat and leave to cool.

3. Preheat the barbecue or griddle pan to hot.

4. When the curry paste has cooled, mix in the slices of chicken and stir to coat.

5. Grill the chicken on the hot barbecue or griddle for 3 minutes on each side. Turn the chicken regularly so that it does not catch.

6. Remove the chicken from the grill, squeeze over the lime juice and garnish with the fresh coriander leaves torn over the top.

how to make
THAI FISHCAKES

makes: 24 * preparation: 10 minutes * cooking: 10 minutes

With this classic Thai street food dish it is important that the fishcakes are tender but not too soft. You can vary the types of fish and flavourings: use more herbs, add curry paste to increase the heat or use a combination of fish and crabmeat or fish and prawn.

 equipment: food processor, mortar and pestle, lightly oiled tray or plate, wok, vegetable oil for deep-frying

*| *

MINCE

500 g white fish fillets in a food processor or blender for a few seconds: a little texture is good so it doesn't have to be completely fine.

POUND

2 garlic cloves, 2 washed and chopped coriander roots, 1 finely sliced shallot, 3 seeded and finely chopped red chillies and a 4 cm piece of peeled and coarsely chopped ginger with ½ teaspoon salt, using a mortar and pestle, until you have a smooth paste.

2

3 TRANSFER

the paste to a bowl with the minced fish and add
1 tablespoon fish sauce. Mix everything together
thoroughly, kneading the mixture with your fingers and
really squeezing it together.

4 PICK UP

a small handful of mixture and throw it firmly against the side of the
bowl with a slap and a flick of the wrist. Repeat the process constantly
for 3–4 minutes. This may sound funny but it makes the fish more
tender as you are breaking down the proteins to tenderise the fish.

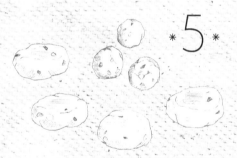

5 LIGHTLY

oil your hands and roll the mixture into 24 balls. When
you are ready to cook, pat the balls into flat cakes about
5 cm wide and 1 cm thick.

6 HEAT

the oil to 200°C in a wok or deep-sided heavy-based pan.
Fry the fishcakes in small batches for 2–3 minutes until
golden brown. Drain on paper towel and serve with
a dipping sauce.

CHEF'S TIP You can keep the shaped fishcakes on an oiled tray in the refrigerator for up
to 12 hours before cooking if you want to prepare them in advance.

Thai fishcakes
with cucumber pickle

This is a great street food dish and perfect to greet your guests with a drink at the beginning of a meal.

serves 6
● ● ● ● ● ●
(makes 24)

preparation
10 minutes

chilling
30 minutes

cooking
10 minutes

fresh

500 g firm white fish fillets
(such as cod or ling)

2 garlic cloves

2 coriander roots, washed and chopped

4 shallots, finely sliced

4 long red chillies, halved, seeded and finely chopped

4 cm piece of ginger, peeled and finely grated

5 kaffir lime leaves, finely chopped

60 g green beans, finely sliced

1 cucumber, finely sliced

juice of 1 lime

4 coriander sprigs, leaves picked and coarsely chopped

pantry/larder

1 teaspoon salt

1 tablespoon fish sauce

75 ml rice vinegar

2 tablespoons caster sugar

2 tablespoons toasted crushed peanuts

vegetable oil, for deep-frying

1. Mince the fish in a food processor or blender for a few seconds: a little texture is good, so it doesn't have to be blended until completely fine.

2. Pound the garlic, coriander roots, 1 of the shallots, 3 of the red chillies, ginger and ½ teaspoon salt using a mortar and pestle until you have a smooth paste. Add to a bowl with the minced fish, fish sauce, kaffir lime leaves and sliced green beans. Thoroughly mix everything together, kneading the mixture with your fingers.

3. Knead the mixture following the instructions on page 47.

4. Lightly oil your hands and roll the mixture into 24 small balls and place them on an oiled tray. Transfer to the refrigerator for 30 minutes.

5. While the fishcakes are chilling, make the cucumber pickle. Warm the vinegar, sugar and salt together in a non-reactive saucepan to melt the sugar. Simmer for 1 minute, then leave to cool. When the vinegar is cool, add the cucumber, remaining shallots and chillies and stir gently. Add the lime juice, chopped coriander and toasted peanuts. Set aside until needed.

6. When ready to fry the cakes, pat them into flat cakes about 5 cm wide and 1 cm thick. Fry the fishcakes following the instructions on page 47. Drain the fishcakes on paper towel and serve with the cucumber pickle.

Fried crab cakes
with coriander

Crabmeat is deliciously sweet and provides a great texture to the standard fishcake.

serves 6
● ● ● ● ● ●
(makes 30)

preparation
10 minutes

chilling
30 minutes

cooking
10 minutes

fresh

300 g firm white fish fillets
(such as cod or ling)

2 garlic cloves, chopped

2 coriander roots, washed and
chopped

3 long green chillies, halved,
seeded and finely chopped

4 cm piece of ginger, peeled and
finely grated

3 spring onions, finely chopped

3 coriander sprigs, leaves picked
and coarsely chopped

3 basil sprigs, leaves picked and
coarsely chopped

300 g cooked, picked crabmeat
(available from supermarkets and
good fish shops)

Sweet chilli sauce (see page 238),
to serve

pantry/larder

½ teaspoon salt

1 tablespoon fish sauce

vegetable oil, for deep-frying

1. Mince the fish in a food processor or blender for a few seconds: a little texture is good, so it doesn't have to be blended completely fine.

2. Pound the garlic, coriander roots, green chillies, ginger and salt using a mortar and pestle until you have a smooth paste. Add to a bowl with the minced fish, fish sauce and spring onions. Thoroughly mix everything together.

3. Knead the mixture following the instructions on page 47. When finished, add the chopped herbs and crabmeat and mix together.

4. Lightly oil your hands, roll the mixture into 30 small balls and place them on an oiled tray. Transfer to the refrigerator for 30 minutes.

5. Fry the crab cakes following the instructions on page 47. Drain them on paper towel and serve with the Sweet chilli sauce.

Salads

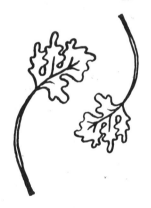

chapter 2

serves 4

• • • •

preparation
10 minutes

Prawn noodle salad
with chilli & toasted cashews

This dish is a visual feast of contrasting colours and textures that looks vibrant and exciting on the plate.

fresh

1 red chilli, seeded and finely chopped

4 cm piece of ginger, peeled and finely grated

juice of 2 limes

250 g cooked thin rice noodles, drained and chilled

250 g cooked prawns, peeled and halved

4 spring onions, finely chopped

4 mint sprigs, leaves picked and torn

4 coriander sprigs, leaves picked and torn

spices

freshly ground black pepper

pantry/larder

2 tablespoons light soy sauce

1 tablespoon blended sesame oil

3 tablespoons toasted cashews

salt

1. Mix the chilli, ginger and lime juice together in a large bowl. Add the light soy sauce and sesame oil. Add the noodles and prawns and mix together. Add the spring onions and season well with a little salt and lots of black pepper.

2. When ready to serve, add the herbs to the noodles and mix together (only add the herbs when you are ready to serve because the acidity of the dressing will turn the leaves black). Scatter with the cashews. Taste the noodles to check the balance of flavours and adjust the seasoning if needed.

Hot & sour grilled beef salad

with toasted rice & coriander

serves 4

● ● ● ●

preparation
10 minutes

cooking
6–8 minutes

All the elements are present in this dish: hot, sweet, salt and sour. The beef is sweet and rich and the dressing is delicious.

fresh

400 g topside of beef

2 long red chillies, seeded and finely chopped

3 spring onions, thinly sliced

½ bunch of coriander, leaves picked

12 mint leaves

juice of 3 limes

spices

freshly ground black pepper

1 teaspoon ground cinnamon

1 teaspoon ground cumin

1 teaspoon ground coriander

pantry/larder

salt

2 tablespoons light soy sauce

4 tablespoons ground toasted rice (see page 17) or toasted sesame seeds

1. Season the beef with salt, black pepper and the ground spices, turning the meat to ensure that it is evenly coated.

2. Preheat a grill, griddle pan or barbecue to hot. Grill the beef for about 6–8 minutes for medium-rare (or longer or shorter if preferred). Rest the meat for 5 minutes, saving all the roasting juices. Slice the beef.

3. Put all the salad ingredients in a serving bowl, toss together with the sliced beef and the saved juices and add the soy sauce.

4. Add half the ground rice or sesame seeds and mix through. Taste to check the balance of flavours and adjust if needed. Garnish with the remaining ground rice or sesame seeds.

CHEF'S TIP

Grilled mushrooms and asparagus could be used as a vegetarian alternative.

serves 6
• • • • • •
(makes 24)

soaking
10 minutes

preparation
10 minutes

cooking
5 minutes

fresh

4 cm piece of ginger, peeled and finely grated

1 tablespoon Sweet chilli sauce (see page 238)

juice of 2 limes

1 cucumber, halved lengthways, seeded, then cut into diagonal strips

3 spring onions, thinly sliced

3 basil sprigs, leaves picked

3 coriander sprigs, leaves picked

½ an aromatic roast duck (available from a Chinese restaurant or some supermarkets), shredded

spices

freshly ground black pepper

pantry/larder

salt

300 g thin glass noodles (wa sun noodles) or rice noodles

2 tablespoons light soy sauce

1 tablespoon blended sesame oil

2 tablespoons toasted sesame seeds

Asian noodle salad
with roast duck & sesame seeds

Roast duck is sweet and rich, but the flavour of lime in this salad will cut through the richness to make a really delicious fresh-tasting salad.

1. Soak the noodles in a bowl of cold water for 10 minutes to soften. Drain, then put the noodles in a saucepan of lightly salted boiling water and cook for about 4 minutes until al dente. Strain, then run under cold water to refresh them.

2. Make a dressing by mixing the ginger, Sweet chilli sauce, lime juice, soy sauce and sesame oil together in a bowl.

3. Mix the noodles, cucumber and spring onions and add a little salt and lots of black pepper.

4. When ready to serve, tear the herbs into the noodles and mix together. Sprinkle with the toasted sesame seeds. Taste the noodles to check the balance of flavours and adjust if needed. Drizzle with the dressing and serve the noodle salad with the roast duck.

Yam som tam
hot & sour green mango salad

serves 4-6
●●●●–●●●●●

preparation
20 minutes

cooking
3–4 minutes

This is a deliciously fresh salad that has variations all over South–East Asia. You will see vendors pounding the ingredients for this taste sensation on pavements, markets and beaches from Hanoi to Singapore.

fresh

2 small bird's eye chillies

2 garlic cloves

2 shallots, thinly sliced

6 cherry tomatoes (the less ripe the better), quartered

juice of 2 limes

1 large unripe green papaya or 2 unripe green mangoes, peeled, stoned and flesh cut into thin matchsticks

a handful of coriander, leaves picked

pantry/larder

2 tablespoons blanched skinless peanuts

a pinch of salt

3 cm piece of palm sugar (or 1 teaspoon soft brown sugar)

1 tablespoon fish sauce

1. Preheat the oven to 170°C. Spread the peanuts out in a roasting tray and roast for about 3–4 minutes until pale golden.

2. Put the chillies, garlic and salt in a mortar and pestle and pound until you have a smooth paste. You can adjust the chilli content if you wish.

3. Add the shallots, cherry tomatoes and palm sugar and pound for 1 minute to break up the ingredients and form a rough paste. Keep turning the mixture over from the bottom as you pound so that the paste gets completely mixed through.

4. Add the lime juice, fish sauce and toasted peanuts. Pound until they are broken up so you will get bits of nuts in every mouthful.

5. Put the papaya or mangoes in a large serving bowl and pour the pounded dressing over. Tear in the coriander leaves. Taste to check the balance of flavours and adjust if needed.

You could add some freshly cooked prawns at the end if you like. This type of salad is great to accompany other dishes such as spice-roast pork or a duck curry.

Grilled prawn & basil salad

serves 4
● ● ● ●

preparation
10 minutes

cooking
4 minutes

Thai basil has an amazing liquorice, aniseed taste and often has flowers and stems with a purple tinge. It is easy to grow the plant from seeds, but it's widely available from Asian grocers and some supermarkets.

fresh

400 g raw prawns, peeled and deveined, tails intact

2 long green chillies, seeded and finely chopped

3 cm piece of ginger, peeled and finely grated

1 lemongrass stem, outer leaves removed, stem finely chopped

2 spring onions, finely chopped

grated zest and juice of 1 lime

juice of 1 orange

3 Thai basil sprigs, leaves picked (or use leaves from 2 regular basil sprigs and 1 mint sprig combined)

spices

freshly ground black pepper

pantry/larder

salt

2 teaspoons grated palm sugar

1 tablespoon fish sauce

1 tablespoon light soy sauce

1. Preheat a griddle pan or grill to high heat. Season the prawns with salt and black pepper. Grill the prawns for 2 minutes on each side until cooked.

2. Put all the fresh ingredients, except the herbs, in a large bowl.

3. Add the palm sugar, fish sauce, soy sauce and the hot grilled prawns and turn them over in the dressing.

4. Leave the salad to cool in the dressing for a few minutes. When you are ready to serve, tear in the Thai basil (or basil and mint), mix together and serve.

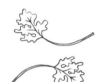

Sesame chicken salad
with white pepper

serves 4
••••

preparation
10 minutes

poaching
20 minutes

cooking
5 minutes

This vibrant salad comes from north-east Thailand. It has great textures and can be a meal in itself accompanied by rice or noodles, or it could be served as part of a larger meal.

fresh

4 coriander sprigs, leaves picked (reserve the stems)

6 celery stalks, from the centre of the bulb

4 cm piece of ginger, peeled and finely chopped (reserve the peel)

3 skinless, boneless chicken breasts

2 garlic cloves, finely chopped

2 green chillies, seeded and finely chopped

4 spring onions, finely chopped

spices

6 white peppercorns

1 teaspoon ground white pepper

pantry/larder

2 tablespoons fish sauce

2 tablespoons rice wine vinegar

¼ teaspoon salt

1 teaspoon caster sugar

2 tablespoons blended sesame oil

2 tablespoons sesame seeds

1. Bring a pan of water to the boil, add the coriander stems, 2 celery stalks, the ginger peelings and the white peppercorns. When the stock is simmering, add the chicken breasts and return it to the boil. Skim the surface to remove any scum that rises to the surface. Simmer the chicken for 5 minutes. Cover the pan with a lid, remove from the heat and stand for 20 minutes: this will result in perfectly cooked, juicy poached chicken. After 20 minutes remove the chicken from the stock and set aside to cool.

2. Cut the remaining celery stalks into thin half-moon slices. Bring a little water to the boil in a small saucepan and parboil the celery for 10 seconds, then refresh under cold running water to stop the cooking. Drain and set aside.

3. Make a dressing by mixing the garlic, chillies and chopped ginger in a bowl with the spring onions, fish sauce, vinegar, salt, sugar and white pepper and set aside for the flavours to infuse while you prepare the chicken.

4. Cut the poached chicken into slices that are about 1 cm wide and 3 cm long. Mix the chicken with the blanched celery and the sesame oil. Add the dressing and set aside for 5 minutes.

5. Meanwhile, set a small frying pan over medium heat and dry-fry the sesame seeds for about 3–4 minutes until they pop and turn golden brown, then remove from the heat.

6. Tear the coriander leaves into the chicken salad and add the toasted sesame seeds. Mix everything together and serve.

Crisp cabbage & coriander salad
with cashews

serves 4
••••

preparation
15 minutes

This salad is a visual feast with many different shades of green on the plate. We enjoy food that looks good and this exciting dish will leave your guests very satisfied.

fresh

1 hard white cabbage, tough outer leaves removed

2 green chillies, seeded and finely chopped

zest and juice of 2 limes

4 cm piece of ginger, peeled and cut into thin matchsticks

4 spring onions, thinly sliced

1 bunch of coriander, leaves picked

½ bunch of mint, leaves picked

pantry/larder

1 tablespoon blended sesame oil

1 tablespoon light soy sauce

1 tablespoon fish sauce

100 g toasted cashews

1. Cut the cabbage into quarters through the central heart. Use a sharp knife to remove the heart from each quarter and discard. Finely shred the cabbage and place in a large bowl.

2. Make a dressing by mixing together the green chillies, lime zest and juice, sesame oil, soy sauce and fish sauce.

3. Mix the shredded cabbage with the ginger, spring onions and the coriander and mint leaves in a large bowl. Add two-thirds of the cashews.

4. When ready to serve, pour the dressing over and toss everything together. Garnish with the remaining cashews.

CHEF'S TIP

Only dress the salad when you are ready to serve, as the dressing is acidic and will turn the herbs black and make the crisp nuts soggy.

Aromatic smoked fish salad

with Asian herbs
& toasted cashews

serves 4-6

●●●―●●●●●

preparation
20 minutes

This is a striking dish to look at: smoking dyes the edges of the fish a yellowy orange, which looks fantastic set against the vibrant, multicoloured salad.

fresh

2 medium-hot red chillies, seeded and finely chopped

juice of 2 limes

2 tablespoons orange juice

3 Aromatic smoked fish, filleted (see page 138)

4 cm piece of ginger, peeled and cut into thin matchsticks

4 spring onions, thinly sliced

4 mint sprigs, leaves picked

4 coriander sprigs, leaves picked

pantry/larder

a pinch of salt

2 tablespoons light soy sauce

1 tablespoon rice vinegar

1 teaspoon blended sesame oil

200 g toasted cashews

1. Pound the chillies with a little salt using a mortar and pestle until you have a smooth paste. Add the lime juice, soy sauce, orange juice, vinegar and sesame oil. Taste the sauce — it should be sour, hot and salty — and adjust if needed.

2. Flake the smoked fish, removing any bones and the grey flesh that is directly behind the skin.

3. Pour the dressing over the fish and add the cashews, ginger and spring onions. Tear in the mint and coriander leaves just before serving.

CHEF'S TIP Oily fish, such as mackerel, rainbow trout or sea mullet, is best for smoking. You could also use a side of salmon. The fish needs to be filleted (get your fishmonger to do this).

Pork & pickled cucumber salad

serves 4-6

●●●●–●●●●●

preparation
20 minutes

cooking
25 minutes

The combination of different flavours and the varying textures that give your jaw and tastebuds a work-out is one of the thrilling things about South–East Asian food. This dish is no exception.

fresh

750 g pork tenderloin

1 large cucumber, halved lengthways, seeded and sliced diagonally

4 shallots, thinly sliced

2 red chillies, seeded and finely chopped

juice of 2 limes

2 coriander sprigs, leaves picked

3 mint sprigs, leaves picked

spices

1 teaspoon five-spice powder

1 teaspoon ground coriander

freshly ground black pepper

pantry/larder

vegetable oil, for cooking

salt

100 g toasted peanuts or cashews

2 tablespoons rice vinegar

1 teaspoon caster sugar

2 tablespoons fish sauce

1. Preheat the oven to 200°C. Put a little oil in a roasting tray set on the stovetop over medium–high heat. Season the pork with all of the spices and some salt. Quickly fry the pork for 2 minutes on each side until browned, then transfer the roasting tray to the oven for 20 minutes until cooked. Remove from the oven and leave to cool.

2. Coarsely crush the peanuts or cashews using a mortar and pestle. Set aside.

3. Heat the vinegar and sugar in a small pan over medium heat, bring to a simmer, then pour it over the cucumber and set aside to cool completely. Add the shallots to the cucumber.

4. Make a dressing by mixing the red chillies with the lime juice and fish sauce. Pour over the cucumber and shallots and toss together.

5. Remove the pork from the roasting tray and transfer to a board. Pour 2 tablespoons of the dressing into the roast pork pan and boil for 30 seconds, stirring with a wooden spoon, to deglaze the pan and pick up all the good bits and juices left by the roasting. Tip this into the rest of the dressing.

6. Slice the pork and add to the cucumber. Tear the coriander and mint leaves into the dressing (only do this when you are ready to serve). Pour the dressing over the meat and cucumber and mix together. Scatter with the crushed nuts and serve.

Crab & lime salad
with coriander & chilli

serves 4-6

●●●●·●●●●●

preparation
10 minutes

This salad is fresh, crisp and delicious.
The crab and cucumber will be sweet or rich
and the fresh mint and coriander provide
a refreshingly delicious bite to the salad.

fresh

2 long red chillies, seeded and
finely chopped

4 cm piece of ginger, peeled and
finely grated

juice of 2 limes

400 g picked white crabmeat
(see Chef's tip)

1 cucumber, halved lengthways,
seeded and sliced diagonally

4 spring onions, thinly sliced

3 mint sprigs, leaves picked

3 coriander sprigs, leaves picked

spices

freshly ground black pepper

pantry/larder

1 tablespoon light soy sauce

2 tablespoons fish sauce

1 teaspoon rice vinegar

salt

1. Make a dressing by mixing the chilli and ginger with the lime
juice, soy sauce, fish sauce and vinegar.

2. Mix the crabmeat, cucumber and spring onions together
in a bowl. Season well with a little salt and lots of black pepper.
Pour the dressing over the crab.

3. Tear the coriander and mint leaves into the salad and mix
everything together, but only add the herbs when you are ready
to serve as the acid will cook the leaves and turn them black.
Taste to check the balance of flavours and adjust if needed
and serve straight away.

CHEF'S TIP

Try to keep the crabmeat in large pieces
so that it is not all mashed up; even when
buying picked crabmeat from a fishmonger,
always check over it to avoid any pieces of
shell that were missed.

serves 4
● ● ● ●

preparation
10 minutes

Roast duck salad
with mango & toasted coconut

Roast duck is delicious with the sweetness and
acidity of fresh mango. The tropical picture
is completed with the addition of some nutty
toasted coconut. What really makes it sing and
pack a hidden punch is the red chilli and raw
ginger. The whole dish is awakened by the
balance of lime juice and soy sauce.

fresh

400 g roast duck meat (available
from a Chinese restaurant or
some supermarkets: about half
a roast duck)

1 mango, peeled, stoned and
sliced

2 limes, pith removed and flesh
chopped from 1, and just the
juice from the other

2 small shallots, finely diced

2 red chillies, seeded and finely
chopped

2 tablespoons toasted shredded
coconut

3 coriander sprigs, leaves picked

3 cm piece of ginger, peeled and
finely grated

8 little gem lettuce leaves
(optional)

pantry/larder

1 tablespoon grated palm sugar

1 tablespoon light soy sauce

1. Shred the roast duck meat into small pieces, tearing it with your
fingers. Mix the duck with the sliced mango, chopped lime, chopped
shallots, red chillies and half the toasted coconut in a bowl. Tear in
the coriander leaves.

2. Make a dressing by mixing the ginger and palm sugar with the
remaining toasted coconut using a mortar and pestle, and pound
to a rough paste. Add the soy sauce and lime juice.

3. Pour the dressing over the duck and toss together. Spoon the
mixture into lettuce leaf cups (if using) or serve with little gem
lettuce as a salad, as a starter or as part of a larger meal.

Prawn noodle salad
with mint & toasted peanuts

serves 4
••••

preparation
15 minutes

This dish is delicious served cold. You could use any combination of seafood instead of just prawns; it is particularly good with crab.

fresh

200 g thin rice noodles, cooked, drained and lightly oiled so that they do not stick together

200 g large cooked prawns, chopped

1 red chilli, seeded and finely chopped

3 cm piece of ginger, peeled and finely grated

juice of 1 lime

2 spring onions, finely chopped

a handful of bean sprouts, washed and trimmed

2 coriander sprigs, leaves picked

spices

freshly ground black pepper

pantry/larder

2 teaspoons grated palm sugar

1 tablespoon tamarind pulp

1 tablespoon fish sauce

2 tablespoons toasted peanuts

salt

1. Mix the cooked noodles and chopped prawns in a large bowl.

2. Make a dressing by mixing the chilli, ginger, palm sugar, lime juice, tamarind and fish sauce together in a small bowl.

3. Pour the dressing over the noodles and prawns. Add the spring onions and bean sprouts and tear in the coriander leaves.

4. When you are ready to serve, crush the peanuts using a mortar and pestle and add to the salad. Season well with salt and black pepper and serve straight away.

Slow roast, smoking grill & hot wok

chapter 3

Kai yang Isaan-style grilled chicken

with black pepper & lemongrass

Kai yang translates as 'grilled chicken' and uses a delicious method of rubbing a paste into the meat, marinating, then grilling slowly so that the flavours caramelise on the skin.

serves 4-6

● ● ● ● - ● ● ● ● ●

preparation
15 minutes

marinating
2 hours

cooking
15 minutes

fresh

4 lemongrass stems, tough outer leaves removed and stems finely chopped

3 coriander roots (or stems), finely chopped

4 garlic cloves

1 long red chilli, seeded and finely chopped

4 chicken thigh fillets, skin on, cut in half

4 boneless chicken breasts, skin on and cut in quarters

Red chilli nam dressing (see page 236), to serve

spices

2 teaspoons freshly ground black pepper

pantry/larder

½ teaspoon salt

1 tablespoon fish sauce

2 teaspoons runny honey

1. Grind the chopped lemongrass with the salt to a rough paste using a mortar and pestle. Add the coriander roots, garlic and chilli and continue to pound. Add the black pepper and keep mixing and pounding until you have a semismooth paste. Add the fish sauce and honey and mix until well blended.

2. Rub the mixture all over the chicken pieces so that they are well coated and leave to marinate in the refrigerator for 2 hours.

3. Preheat a griddle pan or charcoal barbecue: you need the heat to be hot but you are going to cook the chicken slowly to impart a smoky, savoury character and allow the marinade to caramelise on the chicken.

4. If you are using a barbecue, place the chicken on the hot grill in areas that are not too close to the direct heat. Cook slowly for about 15 minutes, turning the chicken every couple of minutes until the chicken is caramelised on the outside and the meat is cooked. Serve with the Red chilli nam dressing.

CHEF'S TIP

If coriander roots are not available, use the lower part of the stems and double the quantity.

Tamarind fried beef
with toasted peanuts

This is a simple and very effective beef dish with an extraordinary balance between different textures and the peppery hot, sweet, salt and sour flavours.

serves 4-6

•••—••••

preparation
10 minutes

marinating
30 minutes

cooking
10 minutes

fresh

2 garlic cloves, finely chopped

2 long red chillies, seeded and finely chopped

4 cm piece of ginger, peeled and finely grated

400 g beef, thinly sliced (topside, rump or part of the sirloin: ask your butcher for a cut of meat that you can cook very quickly and is tender)

1 white onion, thinly sliced

a small handful of coriander, leaves picked and coarsely chopped

spices

freshly ground black pepper

pantry/larder

2 teaspoons light soy sauce

2 teaspoons fish sauce

2 tablespoons tamarind pulp

3 teaspoons granulated sugar

2 tablespoons rice wine vinegar

vegetable oil, for frying

salt

100 g blanched skinless peanuts, toasted and coarsely chopped, to garnish

1. Put the garlic, chillies, ginger, soy sauce, fish sauce and some black pepper in a bowl and mix together. Add the sliced beef and stir to mix and ensure it is evenly coated. Leave to marinate in the refrigerator for 30 minutes.

2. Dissolve the tamarind pulp in 100 ml of water in a small bowl, then transfer to a saucepan. Add 2 teaspoons of the sugar and reduce over medium heat to a thick syrup the consistency of honey.

3. Put the onion in a bowl with the vinegar and remaining sugar. Season with salt, mix together and leave to lightly pickle for 5 minutes.

4. Heat a little oil in a frying pan over medium heat and fry the marinated beef in batches for about 3 minutes until golden brown, then set aside.

5. Mix the coriander with the pickled onions and all the juices, then scatter it over the base of a serving plate. Top with the beef, then pour over the caramelised tamarind syrup and garnish with chopped toasted peanuts.

Thai beef skewers
with red chilli vinegar

serves 4-6

●●●●–●●●●●

preparation
20 minutes

marinating
30 minutes

cooking
10 minutes

This mixture of spices is one of the most ancient in Thai cuisine. The blend of hot, sweet, salt and sour complements the flavour of the beef. It would also work very well with game flavours, such as quail, pheasant, pigeon or even venison.

fresh

400 g tender beef (rump steak, sirloin or rib eye), trimmed of excess fat and sinew and cut into 2–3 cm cubes

3 coriander roots, cleaned and chopped (if not available, use the lower part of the stems, washed and finely chopped)

3 cm piece of ginger, peeled and sliced

Thai red chilli vinegar dressing (see page 232), to serve

a handful of coriander leaves, to garnish (optional)

spices

freshly ground black pepper

20 white peppercorns

½ teaspoon five-spice powder

¼ teaspoon ground turmeric

½ teaspoon ground coriander

pantry/larder

2 tablespoons light soy sauce

pinch of salt

3–4 tablespoons vegetable oil

metal or soaked wooden skewers

1. Mix the soy sauce with a little black pepper in a bowl and add the beef. Stir to ensure it is evenly coated, then set aside to marinate for 30 minutes in the refrigerator.

2. Crush the coriander roots, salt and white peppercorns using a mortar and pestle. Add the ginger and other spices. Continue to pound until well mixed and you have a rough coarsely ground paste.

3. Add the spice mixture to the meat and stir to coat. Thread the coated meat onto the skewers: 3–4 pieces on each skewer.

4. Heat the oil in a wok over a high heat. When hot, add the beef and cook for about 2 minutes on each side until golden brown. Remove the beef from the oil and set aside to rest for a few minutes.

5. Serve with the Thai red chilli vinegar dressing and garnish with coriander leaves (if using). Serve alongside a salad or noodle dish.

CHEF'S TIP

The meat could also be grilled or roasted quickly. Whatever cooking method is used, the meat should be crisp and golden brown on the outside and medium-rare on the inside.

Fragrant chicken wings
with galangal

serves 4-6

●●●–●●●●●

preparation
10 minutes

marinating
1 hour

cooking
8–10 minutes

Chicken wings are the perfect quick snack: they are delicious finger food, especially when covered in a spiced marinade.

fresh

2 garlic cloves, finely chopped

4 coriander roots, cleaned and finely chopped

2 long green chillies, seeded and finely chopped

4 cm piece of galangal (or ginger), peeled and finely grated

700 g chicken wings

lime wedges, to serve

Sweet chilli sauce (see page 238), to serve

spices

1 tablespoon coriander seeds, crushed

½ teaspoon ground cinnamon

½ teaspoon crushed dried chilli

¼ teaspoon ground cardamom

pantry/larder

2 tablespoons fish sauce

1 tablespoon grated palm sugar

1. Mix the garlic, coriander roots, chillies, galangal, all of the spices, fish sauce and palm sugar together in a large bowl.

2. Add the chicken wings and turn to ensure that the wings are all well coated in the marinade. Set aside to marinate for 1 hour in the refrigerator.

3. Preheat a griddle pan or barbecue to hot. Grill the chicken wings for about 8–10 minutes, turning every 2 minutes so that they do not scorch and burn. Cut one chicken wing open to check that it is cooked all the way through. Serve with lime wedges and Sweet chilli sauce.

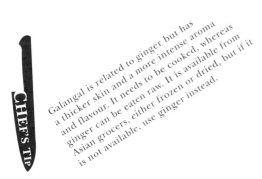

CHEF'S TIP Galangal is related to ginger but has a thicker skin and a more intense aroma and flavour. It needs to be cooked, whereas ginger can be eaten raw. It is available from Asian grocers, either frozen or dried, but if it is not available, use ginger instead.

serves 4
••••

preparation
10 minutes

marinating
1 hour

cooking
8 minutes

fresh

2 garlic cloves, finely chopped

4 cm piece of ginger, peeled and finely grated

4 pork chops

3 mint sprigs, leaves picked

3 coriander sprigs, leaves picked

3 basil sprigs, leaves picked

2 tablespoons bean sprouts, washed and trimmed

2 spring onions, thinly sliced

juice of 2 limes, plus extra wedges to serve

spices

1 tablespoon coriander seeds

1 tablespoon fennel seeds

1 teaspoon ground turmeric

1 teaspoon five-spice powder

½ teaspoon dried chilli flakes

freshly ground black pepper

pantry/larder

1 tablespoon vegetable oil

salt

1 tablespoon blended sesame oil

Barbecued pork & herb salad

These spice-grilled pork chops are rich and delicious. They go really well with a sour dressing and lots of aromatic fresh herbs.

1. Grind the coriander and fennel seeds using a mortar and pestle. Add the garlic and ginger and pound to a paste. Tip the ground mixture into a shallow dish and add the turmeric, five-spice, dried chilli, some black pepper and the vegetable oil. Add the pork chops and rub the marinade into the meat so that the chops are well coated. Set aside to marinate for at least 1 hour in the refrigerator.

2. Preheat a barbecue or griddle pan to hot. When ready to cook, season the pork chops with some salt. Grill the chops for 8 minutes, turning them every 2 minutes so that they do not scorch and burn.

3. Meanwhile, make the salad. Combine the herbs in a bowl and add the beansprouts and spring onions. Dress with the lime juice and sesame oil.

4. When the pork is caramelised and cooked through, set it aside to rest for 5 minutes. Add any juices from the resting meat to the salad, then serve the pork chops with the herb salad and the extra lime wedges for squeezing over.

CHEF'S TIP

Always choose free-range or organic pork as the quality and flavour is superior to intensively farmed pork.

Spiced bavette steak
with hot & sour dressing

serves 4
● ● ● ●

preparation
5 minutes

marinating
30 minutes

cooking
7–8 minutes

Bavette steak is a delicious cut of beef, also known as flap steak. It needs to be cooked medium-rare, then left to rest for 5 minutes before slicing. Ask your butcher for it: you will be amazed and never turn back.

fresh

500 g bavette (flap) steak

12 mint leaves

½ bunch of coriander, leaves picked

1 quantity of Hot and sour red chilli dressing (see page 234)

spices

1 teaspoon ground coriander

½ teaspoon ground cardamom

½ teaspoon ground nutmeg

½ teaspoon crushed dried chilli

1 teaspoon ground ginger

freshly ground black pepper

pantry/larder

salt

1 tablespoon vegetable oil

1. Combine all of the spices in a bowl. Put the beef in a bowl and rub the spice mix all over so that it is evenly coated. Set aside to marinate in the refrigerator for 30 minutes.

2. Preheat a barbecue, griddle pan or frying pan to hot. When ready to cook, season the meat with a little salt, rub with the oil and grill the beef for 2 minutes, then turn the meat over and grill for another 2 minutes. Repeat the process and cook the steak to medium-rare (about 7–8 minutes in total). Set the meat aside to rest for 5 minutes, saving all the roasting juices from the grill pan.

3. Slice the rested beef into 1 cm thick slices across the grain and lay out on a platter. Mix the herbs with the dressing and the roasting juices and pour this over the sliced beef. Taste to check the balance of flavours and add some more dressing if needed.

CHEF'S TIP

Serve with a crisp cabbage salad with toasted cashews or stir-fried greens with garlic and black pepper if you like.

Thai stir-fried beef
with chilli relish

serves 4
● ● ● ●

preparation
15 minutes

cooking
9–11 minutes

Unlike a Chinese stir-fry that would traditionally have soy sauce served as a condiment, a Thai stir-fry is accompanied by the fiery nam pla sauce, which is simply chopped hot bird's eye chillies mixed with fish sauce and a little sugar.

fresh

500 g tender beef, cut into strips for stir-frying

3 tablespoons Thai chilli relish (see page 240)

150 g trimmed green beans or sugar snap peas

4 spring onions, thinly sliced

1 large medium–hot red chilli, seeded and finely chopped

a handful of bean sprouts, washed and trimmed

3 mint sprigs, leaves picked

3 coriander sprigs, leaves picked

juice of 1 lime

steamed rice or noodles, to serve

pantry/larder

2 tablespoons vegetable oil

1. Heat the wok over high heat. Add the oil: it will be smoky so act decisively. Fry a third of the beef, spread out around the pan, for 2–3 minutes until browned and then set aside. Repeat with the remaining beef in two more batches until it is all browned.

2. Return all of the meat to the pan and lower the heat to medium. Add the relish and green beans and simmer for 2 minutes.

3. Add the spring onions and cook for 1 minute so that the vegetables are tender but still crisp.

4. Add the chilli and beansprouts and toss together along with the mint and coriander leaves. Add the lime juice and taste to adjust the seasoning to suite your taste.

5. Serve with steamed rice or noodles as a simple meal or as part of a larger selection of dishes.

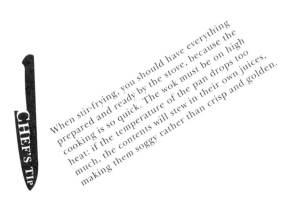

When stir-frying, you should have everything prepared and ready by the stove, because the cooking is so quick. The wok must be on high heat: if the temperature of the pan drops too much, the contents will stew in their own juices, making them soggy rather than crisp and golden.

CHEF'S TIP

Siamese chicken
with ginger, coriander, garlic & white pepper

serves 4-6
••••–•••••

preparation
20 minutes

cooking
10 minutes

Chillies only arrived in Thailand after the Spanish and Portuguese journeyed to South America in the 16th century. Thai dishes that use white pepper are very old and predate the introduction of chillies to Thai cuisine.

fresh

400 g chicken thigh fillets, cut into 2–3 cm cubes

3 coriander roots, cleaned and chopped (if not available, use the lower part of the stems, washed and finely chopped)

4 cm piece of ginger, peeled and finely grated

3 garlic cloves

½ bunch of coriander, leaves picked

spices

20 white peppercorns

1 tablespoon coriander seeds

½ teaspoon ground turmeric

1 tablespoon cumin seeds

pantry/larder

2 tablespoons light soy sauce

pinch of salt

wooden skewers soaked in cold water for at least 30 minutes

1. Marinate the chicken in the light soy sauce while you prepare the rest of the ingredients.

2. Crush the coriander roots, salt and peppercorns using a mortar and pestle. Add the ginger, garlic and the spices and continue to pound until well mixed and you have a coarse ground paste.

3. Add the spice mix to the chicken and rub it all over to ensure it is well coated. Thread 3 pieces of chicken on to each soaked skewer.

4. Preheat a griddle pan or barbecue to hot. Grill the skewers for 2 minutes on each side, then continue to cook for 3–4 minutes until cooked, turning regularly. Alternatively, you can finish cooking the skewers for 5 minutes in an oven preheated to 200°C.

5. Garnish with coriander and serve straight away with a green mango salad.

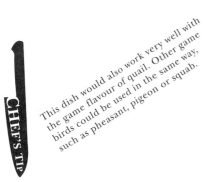

CHEF'S TIP

This dish would also work very well with the game flavour of quail. Other game birds could be used in the same way, such as pheasant, pigeon or squab.

Salt & spice-roast pork belly

serves 4-6
●●●─●●●●

preparation
10 minutes

cooking
1 hour 25 minutes

This has to be one of the best taste combinations in the world. If you don't eat pork, then try this flavour combination on a roasted chicken, a butterflied shoulder of lamb or roast rib of beef.

fresh
1 pork belly, weighing about 1.5–2 kg

Peanut dipping sauce (see page 242), to serve

Crisp cabbage and coriander salad (see page 66), optional

spices
3 tablespoons rock salt

1 tablespoon coriander seeds

1 tablespoon cumin seeds

1 tablespoon fennel seeds

10 white peppercorns

1 teaspoon ground cardamom

1 teaspoon five-spice powder

½ teaspoon dried chilli flakes

pantry/larder
vegetable oil, for rubbing

1. Preheat the oven to 240°C.

2. Pound the rock salt, coriander seeds, cumin seeds, fennel seeds and peppercorns using a mortar and pestle until medium-fine in texture. Add the remaining spices, except the dried chilli flakes, and continue to crush until broken up.

3. Put half of the spice mixture in a high-sided roasting tin and add enough cold water to come 2 cm up the sides of the tin.

4. Score the pork skin into thin strips. Place the pork belly, skin side down, in the water: it should cover the skin and the first deep layer of fat. Put the tin on the stovetop over medium–high heat and bring the water to the boil. Continue to simmer for about 20 minutes. You are simmering the pork in the water to dissolve some of the fat and impart the spicy salt into the skin and make a delicious crackling. After 20 minutes, remove the pork from the water and tip away any of the remaining water.

5. Place the pork belly, skin side up, on a rack in the roasting tin. Mix the dried chilli flakes with the remaining spice mix and rub it into the skin with a little oil.

6. Lower the heat of the oven to 220°C and roast the pork for 20 minutes. Turn the heat down to 180°C and cook for a further 40 minutes until the skin is crispy and the meat is soft and cooked.

7. Serve with the Peanut dipping sauce and a Crisp cabbage and coriander salad (see page 66) if you like.

· 6 ways with ·

CHILLI

 ## Salt & chilli-grilled prawns

Dry-fry 1 tablespoon coriander seeds, 2 teaspoons fennel seeds, 5 star anise and 1 cinnamon stick for 2–3 minutes until fragrant.

Grind the spices until medium-fine in a spice grinder or using a mortar and pestle along with ½ teaspoon black peppercorns and a pinch of chilli flakes.

Season 400 g raw peeled prawns with 3 teaspoons of the ground spice mix and a pinch of coarse salt flakes.

Preheat a barbecue or grill to hot. Grill the prawns for 2 minutes on each side until cooked.

Squeeze the juice of 1 lime over the prawns and garnish with picked coriander.

 ## Prawns & coriander with chilli & tamarind

Heat a splash of vegetable oil in a pan and fry 2 seeded and chopped green chillies and 1 tablespoon of grated ginger.

Fry for about 2 minutes until fragrant and aromatic.

Add 50 g tamarind pulp and 2 tablespoons of light soy sauce.

Remove from the heat and add the juice of 2 limes.

Grill or fry 300 g large raw peeled prawns for about 2 minutes on each side.

Dress the prawns with the chilli tamarind dressing and add the leaves from 3 sprigs of coriander and mint.

 ## Grilled pork with watermelon, lime & dried chilli

Season 1 pork tenderloin and grill under a hot grill for about 12–15 minutes until golden brown and roasted, then set aside to rest for 5 minutes.

Cut half a watermelon into chunks.

Pick the leaves from 3 mint sprigs and tear into the bowl with the watermelon.

Season well with salt. Slice the cooked pork into 5 mm slices and add to the bowl.

Scatter ¼ teaspoon of dried red chilli flakes over the meat: do not be shy with the salt and the chilli. Add the juice of 2 limes.

Mix everything together and taste to check the balance of flavours: make sure you can taste hot chilli, sweet watermelon and some salt and sourness.

 ## Grilled green chilli dip

Grill 4 large whole green chillies, 4 unpeeled garlic cloves and 4 small unpeeled shallots under a hot grill until the skin is charred and the insides are soft.

Peel the blackened skins from the chillies, garlic and shallots when they are cool and then pound them all together using a mortar and pestle.

Squeeze in the juice of 1 lime and 1 tablespoon of fish sauce and mix into the paste. Taste to check the balance of flavours.

Serve with a side plate of some hard-boiled eggs, pieces of cucumber or beside some grilled meat.

 ## Crisp fried chicken patties with green chilli

Chop 300 g skinless chicken breast into 2–3 mm pieces. Mix 2 teaspoons of light soy sauce, 1 teaspoon of oyster sauce and 1 beaten egg in a bowl and add the chicken.

Crush 2 hot green bird's eye chillies, 1 garlic clove and 1 tablespoon of grated ginger together using a mortar and pestle. Add to the chicken and mix together.

Mix 3 finely chopped spring onions and the leaves from 3 sprigs of basil and coriander together well and add to the chicken mixture. Tip the mixture into your hands and firmly slap it back into the bowl. Repeat for 5 minutes to tenderise the meat.

Heat a little vegetable oil in a heavy-based pan. Drop small spoonfuls of the chicken mixture into the hot oil and fry for about 3–4 minutes until golden brown and crispy. Cook in small batches so that the oil stays hot.

 ## Spice-roast pumpkin with honey & chilli

Cut a butternut pumpkin into 3 cm cubes and drizzle with 2 tablespoons of vegetable oil.

Season with a little salt, ½ teaspoon of ground coriander, ½ teaspoon of ground cumin, ½ teaspoon of ground cinnamon and a pinch of cayenne pepper.

Lay out in a roasting tin and roast in an oven preheated to 200°C for 25 minutes until caramelised.

Heat a splash of vegetable oil in a pan and fry 2 chopped red chillies, 1 tablespoon of grated ginger, the grated zest of 1 orange, a pinch of salt and 2 tablespoons of honey until caramelised. Squeeze in the juice of 1 lime.

Pour the fried mixture over the roasted pumpkin and garnish with lime wedges and torn coriander leaves.

Slow-roasted pork shoulder

with coriander, tamarind & chilli

serves 6
● ● ● ● ●

preparation
10 minutes

cooking
6 hours

resting
15 minutes

fresh

3 cm piece of ginger, peeled and grated

1 free-range pork shoulder, butterflied, scored and rolled (ask your butcher to do this for you), weighing about 2 kg

1 red chilli, seeded and finely chopped

spices

1 teaspoon black peppercorns

½ teaspoon cloves

½ teaspoon ground cardamom

1 tablespoon fennel seeds

2 tablespoons coriander seeds

5 star anise

2 cinnamon sticks

½ teaspoon freshly grated nutmeg

½ teaspoon dried chilli flakes

pantry/larder

2 teaspoons salt

3 tablespoons tamarind pulp

1 tablespoon blended sesame oil

1 tablespoon light soy sauce

1 tablespoon honey

The best cut of pork to slow roast is a shoulder, as it is layered with meat and fat. The longer the meat roasts, the slower the fat melts, keeping the meat really juicy.

1. Preheat the oven to 180°C.

2. Put all the spices and the salt in a spice blender or electric coffee grinder with the ginger and blitz until fine. Any spices that you do not use, store in an airtight container for next time.

3. Rub the spice blend into the scored skin of the pork shoulder, ensuring it is rubbed into all the crevices. Place the meat in a roasting tin and add 200 ml of water to the bottom of the tin. Roast in the oven for 30 minutes to start the pork meat cooking. Reduce the temperature to 140°C and slow cook for another 5 hours. Check the meat regularly and pour all the roasting juices back over the meat. Do not let the crackling scorch or burn.

4. Remove the meat from the oven and tip all the roasting juices into a jug. Spoon off the clear pork fat and keep the darker roasting juices. Add the tamarind pulp, sesame oil, soy sauce, honey and chopped red chilli to the jug and mix together.

5. Increase the oven temperature to 180°C. Pour the tamarind honey dressing over the pork and return the tin to the oven for 30 minutes. Baste the meat with the pan juices 2–3 times to ensure the crackling does not scorch. Leave the meat to rest for 15 minutes before carving; however, it will be more like pulling it apart as the meat will be so soft. Serve with a crisp salad and Braised mushrooms (see page 192) if you like.

Wok-fried chilli & basil chicken

serves 4

●●●●

(as part of a
large meal)

preparation
10 minutes

cooking
7–8 minutes

This is a simple stir-fry that could be eaten on its own or as part of a larger Asian meal where a number of dishes are served in a continuous seamless flow from the kitchen to the table.

fresh

4 cm piece of ginger, peeled and finely grated

2 boneless, skinless chicken breasts, cut into 1 cm slices

2 garlic cloves

2 red chillies, seeded and finely chopped

200 g snow peas

4 spring onions, thinly sliced

3 coriander sprigs, leaves picked

3 basil sprigs, leaves picked

juice of 1 lime

spices

freshly ground black pepper

pantry/larder

2 tablespoons vegetable oil

salt

1 tablespoon light soy sauce

1½ tablespoons fish sauce

1. Heat a wok over medium–high heat. Add half the oil and fry the ginger for 1 minute until fragrant.

2. Add the sliced chicken and fry briskly, spreading it out around the wok so that the slices are in contact with the maximum amount of heat. Fry for 3–4 minutes until golden brown, then season with salt and black pepper.

3. Add the remaining oil and fry the garlic and the chillies for about 1–2 minutes until fragrant, then add the snow peas.

4. Add the spring onions with the soy sauce and fish sauce and stir-fry for 1 more minute. Stir in the coriander and basil leaves together with the lime juice and serve.

Whole spice-roast poussin
with lemongrass & coconut cream

serves 4
••••

preparation
15 minutes

cooking
40 minutes

This dish has an intense depth of flavour that comes from the use of aromatic spices such as lemongrass, ginger and galangal. Once tried, it will soon become a firm favourite.

fresh

2 small onions, finely diced

2 garlic cloves, crushed

4 cm piece of ginger, peeled and left whole

2 cm piece of galangal, peeled and left whole (see tip below)

4 poussins (spring chickens)

4 lemongrass stems, tough outer leaf removed and stems bruised with the back of a heavy knife

juice of 2 limes

pantry/larder

4 dried chillies, soaked in hot water to soften, then water discarded

1 teaspoon salt

300 ml coconut cream

2 teaspoons grated palm sugar

1. Preheat the oven to 200°C.

2. Put the onions, garlic, ginger and galangal in a food processor and blend to a paste. Add the soaked chillies, salt and a little water and continue to blend to a smooth paste.

3. Stuff each poussin with the bruised lemongrass and then rub the spice mixture inside and out.

4. Place any remaining spice mixture in a saucepan with the coconut cream and palm sugar and heat over medium–high heat. Bring to the boil, then simmer until it has reduced by half.

5. Preheat a grill or grill pan to hot. Place the poussin on the hot grill and grill for 3–4 minutes on all sides. Transfer the poussin to a roasting tin and roast for 20 minutes. Baste the poussin with the coconut mixture every 5 minutes until the poussin is tender and the coconut spice mixture is all used up.

6. Pour all the juices from the pan over the poussin and finish with the lime juice. Serve with a rice or noodle dish.

If galangal is not available, use double the amount of ginger.

Sweet & crispy pork spare ribs

Pork spare ribs are always a favourite: everyone likes gnawing on delicious bone. This recipe comes from Phuket in the south of Thailand and is very tasty.

serves 6
● ● ● ● ● ●

preparation
10 minutes

marinating
2 hours

cooking
6–8 minutes
(per batch)

fresh

2 garlic cloves, finely chopped

3 coriander roots, finely chopped

500 g pork spare ribs, cut into short lengths (ask your butcher to do this)

Green chilli nahm jim (see page 237), to serve

spices

2 teaspoons white peppercorns

2 teaspoons black peppercorns

1 tablespoon coriander seeds

5 star anise

pantry/larder

1 tablespoon soft brown sugar

1 tablespoon dark soy sauce

1 tablespoon fish sauce

1 tablespoon honey

2 tablespoons rice flour

vegetable oil, for deep-frying

1. Crush the white and black peppercorns, coriander seeds and star anise using a mortar and pestle, and continue to work until you have a medium–fine powder. Add the garlic, coriander roots and brown sugar and continue to pound to a paste. Add the soy sauce, fish sauce and honey and mix together.

2. Place the ribs in a bowl and pour the spice mixture over. Rub all over so that the ribs are well coated, then set aside to marinate for 2 hours in the refrigerator to impart all the great flavours.

3. Place the rice flour in a shallow dish. Remove the ribs from the marinade, dip them in the flour to coat, then dust off any excess.

4. Heat the oil for frying in a wok to 200°C, or until a cube of bread dropped in browns in 15 seconds. Deep-fry the ribs in small batches for 6–8 minutes until they are a deep golden brown. Remove with a slotted spoon and drain on paper towel. Serve with Green chilli nahm jim.

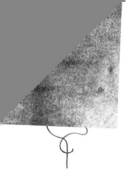

Caramelised chilli roast chicken

serves 4-6
●●●●–●●●●●

preparation
10 minutes

marinating
1 hour

cooking
15 minutes

Roast chicken with crispy skin, caramelised sticky chilli dressing, something that you can hold in your fingers and devour… need I say more? Lots of paper napkins needed.

fresh
8–12 chicken drumsticks, skin on
1 quantity of Chilli tamarind caramel (see page 235)
lime wedges, to serve

spices
1 teaspoon ground cinnamon
½ teaspoon ground white pepper
½ teaspoon allspice
½ teaspoon ground coriander
½ teaspoon ground turmeric
freshly ground black pepper

pantry/larder
1 tablespoon vegetable oil
salt

1. Use a sharp knife to score 3 deep cuts into each chicken drumstick, right down to the bone. This will ensure that the marinade gets all the way through the meat and that they cook quicker so the meat stays moist and juicy.

2. Mix all the spices with some black pepper and the oil in a small bowl. Place the drumsticks in a shallow dish and pour over the marinade. Set aside to marinate in the refrigerator for at least 1 hour.

3. Preheat the oven to 200°C. Put a sheet of baking paper on a baking tray and lay the chicken on top. Season with salt and roast for 10 minutes until three-quarters cooked.

4. Remove the chicken from the oven and pour over half the Chilli tamarind caramel. Return to the oven to roast for another 5 minutes.

5. When the chicken drumsticks are caramelised, roasted and delicious, serve with lime wedges and the remaining Chilli tamarind caramel for dipping.

Fish & seafood

chapter 4

Spice-fried squid

serves 4-6

●●●●–●●●●●

preparation
15 minutes

soaking
1 hour

cooking
1 minute

Squid, prawns and other sweet seafood lend themselves very well to being fried with a hot and salty coating. It could be salt and pepper or salt and chilli or a combination of crushed pepper, dried chilli and sichuan pepper: they are all delicious and make a great snack.

fresh

500 g squid

150 ml milk, for soaking

5 cm piece of ginger, peeled and finely grated

1 red chilli, seeded and finely chopped

coarsely chopped coriander leaves, to serve

lime wedges, to serve

pantry/larder

3 tablespoons rice flour

3 teaspoons Salt and pepper mix (see page 246)

vegetable oil, for deep-frying

1. Prepare the squid as described below. Use a sharp knife to score the inside of the squid tube in a crisscross pattern, running the knife from side to side, making sure that you do not cut all the way through. Then cut the tube into 3 cm x 5 cm pieces.

2. Soak the squid in the milk for at least 1 hour to tenderise. When ready to cook, remove the squid from the milk and pat dry with paper towel.

3. Put the ginger, red chilli, rice flour and the Salt and pepper mix in a bowl and mix together. Add the squid to the bowl and stir to make sure the pieces are fully coated.

4. Fill a wok one-quarter full with vegetable oil and heat over medium–high heat to 180°C (see tip below). Shake the excess flour from the squid pieces, then carefully add them to the hot oil. Cook for 1 minute, then remove with a slotted spoon and drain well on paper towel. Serve garnished with coriander and lime wedges.

* how to *
PREPARE SQUID

* *Pull out the tentacles, then pull off the side flaps of the squid. The squid tubes have a natural seam that runs down one side. Use a sharp knife to split them open; scrape off any jelly-like substance and discard.*

* *Remove the outer skin from the squid and discard.*

* *Holding the tentacles, take your thumb and finger in front of the ink sack and push towards the tentacles. There is a small hard beak that will be exposed: remove this and discard, then cut between the ink sack and the tentacles. You will be left with the opened out tubes and the tentacles. Wash them in cold running water, then pat dry with paper towel.*

CHEF'S TIP

To check that the oil is ready for frying, drop in a small piece of bread: it should turn golden in about 15 seconds.

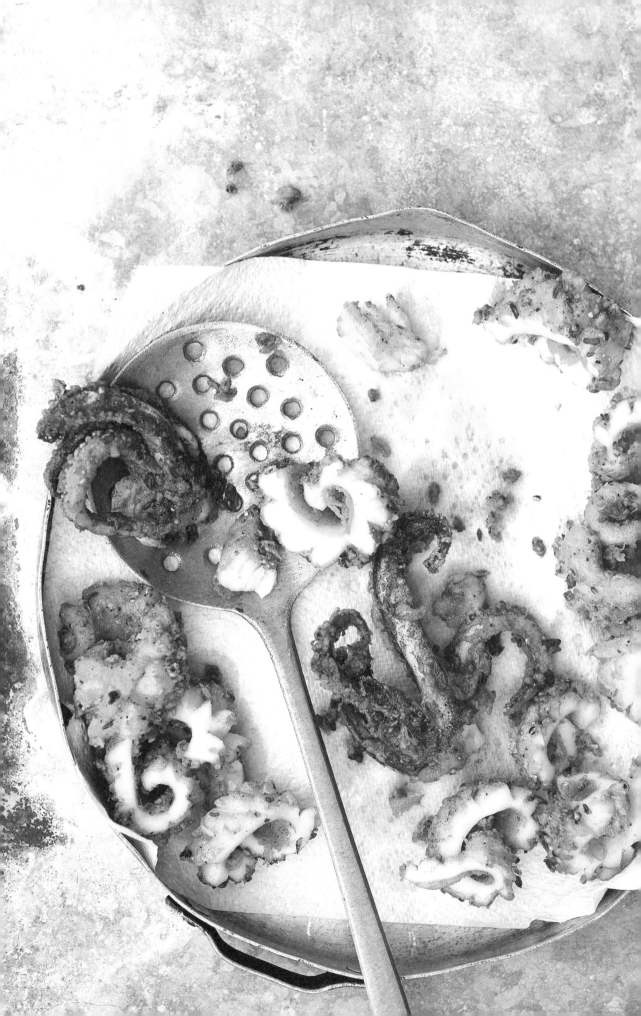

serves 4-6
●●●–●●●●●

preparation
10 minutes

cooking
1–2 minutes

fresh

1 garlic clove

two 4 cm pieces of ginger, peeled

4 medium–hot green chillies, seeded and finely chopped

1 large bunch of coriander, leaves and stems coarsely chopped, plus 3 extra sprigs, leaves picked and chopped, to garnish

juice of 2 limes

18 large scallops

3 spring onions, finely chopped

spices

freshly ground black pepper

pantry/larder

2 tablespoons blanched skinless cashews, toasted

2 tablespoons blanched skinless peanuts, toasted

½ teaspoon caster sugar

½ teaspoon salt, plus extra to taste

3 tablespoons coconut cream

2 tablespoons vegetable oil

12–18 scallop shells, cleaned, to serve (optional)

Grilled scallops
with green cashew relish

The bright green of this sauce is very vivid and is a great combination of different flavours and textures.

1. Set aside half the cashews to garnish the finished dish. Put the remaining nuts in a food processor and add the garlic, 1 piece of the ginger and the sugar and salt and process to a paste. Add the green chilli and coriander and blend again. Add the coconut cream and 2 tablespoons of water and blend together — not too smooth as you want a bit of texture.

2. Transfer the paste to a bowl and add the lime juice. Taste to check the balance of flavours and adjust the seasoning if needed.

3. Clean the scallops by removing the small opaque muscle from the side, which will be attaching the fish to the shell. The orange-coloured roe can be left on or removed, depending on your taste. Place the scallops on layers of paper towel to dry.

4. Meanwhile, thinly slice the remaining ginger, restack the slices and finely shred into thin needles. Crush the remaining nuts.

5. Preheat the griddle pan or barbecue to hot. When the scallops are dry, season them with salt and black pepper. Oil the pan or barbecue and grill the scallops for 60–80 seconds on each side, depending on the thickness. To turn the scallops quickly, use two dessert spoons, one in each hand, and flick the scallops over from one spoon to the other. When the scallops are grilled on both sides, remove from the grill.

6. Place a scallop in each shell (if using). Spoon over a little green cashew relish, scatter with some shredded ginger and spring onions, then some crushed nuts and coriander leaves. Serve immediately.

* THAI *
knife techniques

Many of the ingredients in Thai cooking are very pungent or aromatic, are often eaten raw in the form of a garnish and can often be very fibrous, tough or woody. This means that you have to chop a lot of these ingredients very finely. For this reason you need to have a good large cook's knife and make sure it is really sharp.

GINGER

When choosing ginger, select the freshest looking and juiciest. If the outside is dry and bark-like, then the flesh inside is going to be tough and woody. Always buy more ginger than you will need as it keeps and you never know what the inside is really like so you may need some more.

Use a large sharp cook's knife. Peel the ginger, cutting away the peel and straightening the edges (keep all the trimmings as you can use them for curry pastes).

Use the sharp knife to cut the ginger into thin slices, aiming to get them as thin as possible.

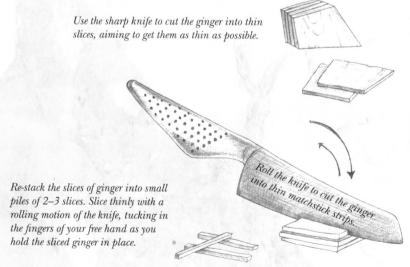

Re-stack the slices of ginger into small piles of 2–3 slices. Slice thinly with a rolling motion of the knife, tucking in the fingers of your free hand as you hold the sliced ginger in place.

Roll the knife to cut the ginger into thin matchstick strips.

This shredded ginger can be used to garnish salads and curries and is visually very appealing. You can also grate the ginger but it will not look quite as nice.

FRESH KAFFIR LIME LEAVES

It is important that fresh kaffir lime leaves are cut very finely as they are not palatable if you come across a large chunk in a dish. This technique is used again and again in Thai cooking. If leaves are not available, use fresh lime zest, which provides some of the aromatic qualities of shredded leaves.

On the back of the kaffir lime leaves there is a raised stem. Use a sharp knife to shave the stem from the leaf so that the leaves are flat.

Tightly roll the leaves into a thin firm cigar. Working the knife rhythmically with a rolling motion, finely shred the leaves into thin needle-like threads, aiming to get these as fine as possible.

CHILLIES

The seeds and white membrane are the hottest part of the chilli. If you remove these then you have a bit more control of the heat of the chilli.

To seed long red or green chillies cut the tops off and discard.

Place the knife parallel to the board at the tip of the chilli and use your free hand to lightly hold the chilli in place. Carefully move the knife through the centre of the chilli using the whole of the blade from the tip, cutting the chilli in half.

When halved, repeat this exaggerated sawing motion of the knife and run it from the tip of the chilli to the base, slicing out all of the seeds and the white pith. Discard all the pith and seeds and clean the board.

Group 2–3 halves of chilli, inside flesh uppermost, and thinly slice with a rolling motion of the knife.

Grilled fish
with chilli tamarind caramel

This intense rich caramel goes very well with the sweet taste of the fish.

serves 4
● ● ● ●

preparation
5 minutes

marinating
10 minutes

cooking
6 minutes

fresh

4 coriander roots, finely chopped

1 red chilli, seeded and finely chopped

4 cm piece of ginger, peeled and finely grated

juice of 1 lime

4 fillets of fish, skin on (sea bream, snapper, sea mullet or even rainbow trout)

1 quantity of Chilli tamarind caramel (see page 235)

2 coriander sprigs, leaves picked, to garnish

spices

freshly ground black pepper

pantry/larder

salt

2 tablespoons flaked coconut, toasted

1. Pound the coriander roots with the red chilli and a pinch of salt using a mortar and pestle. Add the grated ginger and the lime juice.

2. Lay the fish fillets in a shallow dish and spread the paste all over them. Set aside to marinate for 10 minutes in the refrigerator.

3. Preheat a grill or a griddle pan to hot. Season the marinated fish with salt and black pepper. If using a griddle pan, grill the fish, skin side down, first. If using an overhead grill, cook the fish skin side up. Grill for 3 minutes on each side, then remove to a serving platter, serving the fish skin side up, which should be blistered and golden brown.

4. Spoon over some of the Tamarind chilli caramel and garnish with the toasted coconut and coriander.

serves 4
● ● ● ●

preparation
10 minutes

cooking
3 minutes

Sesame-seared tuna
with lemongrass & ginger

The dressing for this dish is packed full of flavour, colour and texture and works brilliantly with the seared tuna.

fresh

3 cm piece of ginger, peeled and finely grated

2 lemongrass stems, tough outer leaves removed and stems thinly sliced

grated zest and juice of 3 limes

grated zest and juice of 1 orange

4 spring onions, thinly sliced

2 green chillies, seeded and finely chopped

400 g tuna, cut into 4 steaks

10 mint leaves, finely chopped

3 coriander sprigs, leaves picked and coarsely chopped

spices

freshly ground black pepper

pantry/larder

salt

2 tablespoons light soy sauce

3 tablespoons sesame seeds

1 tablespoon vegetable oil

salt

1. Mix the ginger, lemongrass, lime and orange zest and juice, soy sauce, spring onions and chillies together in a bowl.

2. Season the tuna steaks with salt and black pepper and sprinkle with the sesame seeds.

3. Preheat a frying pan over high heat. When hot, add the vegetable oil. Sear the tuna steaks for 90 seconds on each side.

4. Remove the tuna from the pan and place them in the marinade. Mix in half the herbs.

5. Serve the tuna with the marinade spooned over the top of the fish and garnish with remaining herbs.

CHEF'S TIP

Make sure that your tuna is from a sustainable source; try to use albacore or skipjack or a smaller species of tuna.

Crispy fried whitebait
with Thai spices

serves 4
● ● ● ●

preparation
5 minutes

marinating
5 minutes

cooking
3 minutes
(per batch)

Whitebait are tiny little fish that you deep-fry whole and are the perfect snack or starter to any meal. You could also use fresh anchovies or sardines.

fresh

500 g whitebait, cleaned

juice of 1 lime

2 lemongrass stems, tough outer leaves removed and stems finely chopped

4 cm piece of ginger, peeled and finely grated

coriander leaves, to serve

lime wedges, to serve

Hot and sour red chilli dressing (see page 234), Fresh chilli jam (see page 239) or Green chilli nahm jim (see page 237), to serve

pantry/larder

200 ml vegetable oil

1 tablespoon fish sauce

3 teaspoons Salt and pepper mix (see page 246)

100 g rice flour

I. Preheat the vegetable oil in a wok to 200°C, or until a cube of bread dropped in browns in 15 seconds.

2. Put the whitebait in a bowl with the lime juice and fish sauce. Add the lemongrass, ginger and the Salt and pepper mix and mix to ensure all the whitebait are coated. Set aside for 5 minutes to absorb all the flavours.

3. Put the rice flour in a shallow dish or plate and tip the whitebait into the flour, shaking off any excess. Make sure that the small fish are coated in the flour, then transfer them to a sieve to shake off any excess flour.

4. When the oil is hot, deep-fry the whitebait in small batches for about 3 minutes until golden brown. Drain the fried fish on paper towel, garnish with torn coriander leaves and serve with lime wedges and the Hot and sour red chilli dressing, Fresh chilli jam or Green chilli nahm jim.

CHEF'S TIP

This marinade and dressing could be used for any fish or shellfish, such as prawns or squid.

Turmeric grilled fish

serves 4-6
●●●—●●●●●

preparation
20 minutes

marinating
20 minutes

cooking
9–10 minutes

You can use any small- to medium-sized fish
for this dish, allowing one fish per person.
Alternatively, you could use a whole large fish
for a number of people.

fresh

2 limes, plus extra lime wedges
to serve

4 red chillies, seeded

2 lemongrass stems, tough outer
leaves removed and stems finely
chopped

4 cm piece of ginger, peeled and
finely grated

4 shallots, chopped

1 whole fish (such as sea bream,
sea bass or snapper), weighing
about 1 kg, cleaned (or use
4–6 smaller fish if preferred)

spices

1 teaspoon ground turmeric

pantry/larder

1 teaspoon salt

200 ml coconut cream

1. Use a sharp knife to cut the skin and pith from the limes,
then finely chop the flesh.

2. Put the chillies and salt in a mortar and pestle and start to grind
together. Add the lemongrass and ginger and work into a paste. Add
the shallots and diced lime flesh, then add a little of the coconut
cream to bring the paste together.

3. Transfer the marinade to a wide bowl with the remaining
coconut cream and the ground turmeric and mix together.

4. Cut 3 diagonal slits in each side of the fish, cutting down to
the bone to allow the marinade to penetrate right into the centre.
Add the fish to the marinade and turn so that the whole fish is well
coated. Set aside to marinate for 20 minutes in the refrigerator,
turning regularly so that the fish is evenly coated.

5. Preheat a barbecue or griddle pan to hot. Fold a large piece
of foil in half and lay it on the grill. Lay the fish on the foil and grill
for 5–6 minutes on each side, basting frequently with any leftover
marinade until browned and cooked.

6. Serve immediately, with lime wedges, as a snack, starter
or as part of larger meal.

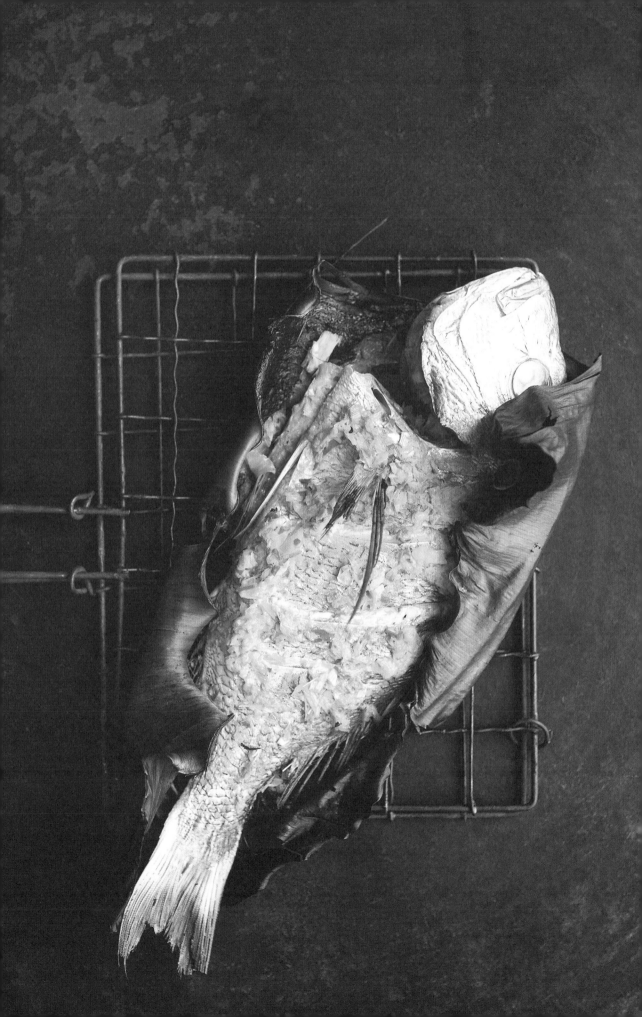

Miang pla thuu

Thai salad of mackerel with ginger, shallots & lime

serves 6
● ● ● ● ● ●

preparation
10 minutes

cooking
6 minutes

Any oily fish that has a sweet taste can be used for this simple salad. The flavours are quite intense, so it is best eaten as an appetiser.

fresh

700 g fish fillets (mackerel, members of the tuna family, swordfish, kingfish or rainbow trout), skin on

2 limes

2 medium–hot green chillies, seeded and finely chopped

4 cm piece of ginger, peeled and finely grated

4 shallots, thinly sliced

crisp lettuce leaves, to serve

spices

freshly ground black pepper

pantry/larder

salt

vegetable oil, for cooking

2 tablespoons fish sauce

2 teaspoons soft brown sugar

100 g blanched skinless peanuts, toasted and crushed

1. Heat a heavy-based frying pan over medium–high heat. Season the fish with salt and black pepper. Add a little oil to the pan and cook the fish, skin side down, for 3 minutes. Turn the fish over and cook for another 3 minutes until the flesh is golden brown and cooked through: you may need to cook for longer depending on the cut of fish. Remove the fish from the pan and set aside to cool.

2. Zest one of the limes, then use a sharp knife to remove the white pith from the lime and discard. Cut the flesh of the lime into thin slices and then finely chop, removing any thick white pieces of membrane. Juice the remaining lime into a large bowl and mix with the fish sauce and the brown sugar to make a dressing.

3. Flake the fish into the dressing, removing any bones or pieces of skin as you go. Add the chillies, chopped lime, ginger, shallots and the lime zest and mix together gently to avoid breaking the fish into a pulp. Taste the mixture and adjust accordingly: it should be hot, sweet, salty and sour. Mix in the crushed peanuts and spoon the mixture into the crisp lettuce leaves to serve.

Stir-fried cod
with sugar snap peas, ginger & five-spice

serves 4
● ● ● ●
(as part of a
large meal)

preparation
10 minutes

cooking
8 minutes

fresh

4 cm piece of ginger, peeled and cut into thin slices

200 g sugar snap peas, trimmed

2 garlic cloves, finely chopped

3 coriander roots, cleaned and finely chopped

1 red chilli, seeded and finely chopped

600 g cod (or other firm white fleshed fish, such as ling), cut into 2 cm cubes

4 spring onions, finely chopped

juice of 1 lime

3 coriander sprigs, leaves picked

spices

freshly ground black pepper

1 teaspoon five-spice powder

½ teaspoon ground coriander

½ teaspoon ground cinnamon

pantry/larder

salt

2 tablespoons vegetable oil

1½ tablespoons fish sauce

1 tablespoon soy sauce

This is a simple stir-fry that is packed full of flavour. Stir-fries from China and South–East Asia often feature a couple of prominent ingredients, such as ginger and chilli.

1. Heat a wok over medium–high heat. Add half the oil and fry the ginger for 1 minute until fragrant. Add the sugar snap peas, spreading them out around the wok so that they are in contact with the heat. Fry for 2 minutes, season with salt and black pepper, then use a slotted spoon to remove them from the wok.

2. Add the remaining oil and fry the garlic, coriander roots and chilli for about 1 minute until fragrant, then add the fish. Season with the dried spices and cook for 2 minutes until the fish has browned. Add the fish sauce and soy sauce and stir-fry until bubbling.

3. Return the peas and the ginger to the wok, add the spring onions and mix together. Squeeze the lime juice over and serve garnished with the coriander leaves.

Aromatic smoked fish

This is a simple way of transforming the flavour of a delicate fish. Other fish or shellfish can be used, with oily ones being the best choice (mackerel, salmon, trout, tuna or prawns).

serves 4-6
•••• - ••••••

preparation
15 minutes

marinating
20 minutes

smoking
12–15 minutes

fresh

juice of 1 lime

500 g fish, for smoking (oily fish, such as mackerel, rainbow trout, salmon or sea mullet are good, but any fish fillet will work)

2 lemongrass stems, coarsely chopped

4–5 cm piece of ginger, peeled and coarsely chopped

spices

freshly ground black pepper

4 star anise

4 cinnamon sticks

1 tablespoon fennel seeds, crushed

1 tablespoon coriander seeds, crushed

pantry/larder

3–4 tablespoons soft brown sugar

2 tablespoons light soy sauce

100 g uncooked white Thai rice

50 g jasmine tea or green tea (teabags are fine)

100 g desiccated coconut

1. Combine 2 teaspoons of the brown sugar, soy sauce, lime juice and some black pepper in a shallow dish. Add the fish fillets and turn so they are coated. Set aside to marinate for about 20 minutes in the refrigerator.

2. Line a large wok with two layers of foil. Combine all of the remaining ingredients in the wok. Set a wire rack on top of the wok.

3. Place the fillets on top of the rack and cover with a lid.

4. Start the heat on medium–high so that the smoking mix starts to caramelise for 2 minutes, then turn down the heat. Smoke the fish for 12–15 minutes, turning once while smoking. When cooked, remove the fish and set aside to cool. When the fish is cool, remove the skin and bones and grey blood line before serving.

5. This hot smoked fish will keep like a cooked piece of fish for about 3 days in the refrigerator.

CHEF'S TIP
The fish or shellfish can be smoked a couple of days in advance, and can be used for salads or other dishes. If you are smoking a larger fish then it may take a little longer to smoke and cook.

Tea-smoked trout
with toasted coconut & ginger

serves 4

• • • •

(as a starter)

preparation
10 minutes

cooking
10 minutes

Fillets of rainbow trout are great for hot smoking with an aromatic smoking mix as the fish is cheap to buy and has a good oil content. The smoking imparts a beautiful aroma to the fish.

fresh

4 cm piece of ginger, peeled and finely grated

1 red chilli, seeded and finely chopped

4 Aromatic smoked fish fillets (see page 138)

1 quantity of Fresh chilli jam (see page 239)

2 mint sprigs, leaves picked

juice of 2 limes

spices

1 tablespoon coriander seeds, crushed

pantry/larder

50 g dried flaked coconut

1. Put the flaked coconut, crushed coriander seeds, ginger and red chilli into a dry frying pan. Cook slowly over medium heat for about 4 minutes until the coconut and coriander is toasted, fragrant and golden brown. The ginger and chilli will dry out and also become fragrant.

2. Flake the smoked fish into large chunks and arrange them on individual plates or a large platter.

3. Dollop some Fresh chilli jam over the fish. Tear the mint leaves and add them to the fried mixture. Scatter the coconut, ginger and mint garnish over the top and squeeze the lime juice over. Serve straight away.

serves 4-6
●●●●–●●●●●

preparation
10 minutes

cooking
1 minute

Rare grilled tuna
with Asian herb dressing

Serve these little cubes of tuna as an appetiser with cold drinks before a meal or as one of the starter courses.

fresh

2 red chillies, seeded and finely chopped

2 spring onions, finely chopped

grated zest and juice of 2 limes

500 g tuna, cut into 3 steaks

2 coriander sprigs, leaves picked

2 Thai basil sprigs, leaves picked (or use regular basil)

pantry/larder

1 tablespoon coriander seeds

¼ teaspoon ground black pepper, plus extra for seasoning

to serve

2 tablespoons fish sauce

2 teaspoons blended sesame oil

vegetable oil, for frying

salt

1. Dry-roast the coriander seeds in a frying pan over medium heat, then coarsely crush them using a mortar and pestle.

2. Combine all of the ingredients except the tuna and herbs in a bowl and mix well to make a dressing. Set aside.

3. Heat a non-stick frying pan over high heat and add a little vegetable oil.

4. Season the tuna with salt and black pepper. Sear the tuna for 40 seconds on each of the 4 sides, turning the tuna chunks with a pair of kitchen tongs.

5. Remove the tuna from the pan and set on a chopping board. Use a coarse-toothed, serrated bread knife to slice the tuna into thin slices, then arrange them on a large platter.

6. Spoon the dressing over and scatter the coriander and basil leaves over the top to finish.

Marinated prawn satay

serves 4-6
•••-•••••

preparation
10 minutes

marinating
1 hour

cooking
10 minutes

Prawn paste, used in this dish, is available from any Asian grocery store and has a strong pungent smell when raw; however, when you cook the paste it loses its pungency and becomes more aromatic.

fresh

2 garlic cloves, finely chopped

juice of 1 lime, plus extra lime wedges to serve

1 kg large raw prawns, peeled and deveined, heads and tails intact

spice

½ teaspoon dried chilli flakes

pantry/larder

2 tablespoons blanched skinless peanuts

pinch of salt

1 tablespoon vegetable oil

1 teaspoon prawn paste
(see page 18)

100 ml coconut cream

1 packet of 15 cm wooden bamboo skewers, soaked in cold water for 30 minutes

1. Dry-fry the peanuts in a frying pan over medium–high heat until golden brown, keeping the peanuts moving so that they do not scorch. Transfer them to a mortar and pestle and finely grind.

2. Work the garlic into a paste with the salt and dried chilli flakes on a clean chopping board or using a mortar and pestle.

3. Heat the vegetable oil in a pan over medium–high heat. Fry the garlic paste with the prawn paste until fragrant and aromatic, then add the lime juice and coconut cream and stir together. Simmer gently over low heat for 4–5 minutes. Taste the mixture and adjust the seasoning if needed: it should be hot, sweet, salty and cut with the sourness of the lime. Set the paste aside to cool.

4. Once the paste has cooled, add the prawns and set aside to marinate for at least 1 hour in the refrigerator.

5. Preheat a griddle pan or barbecue to hot. Thread 3–4 marinated prawns onto the soaked bamboo skewers. Grill the prawns on the griddle pan or barbecue for a couple of minutes on each side, then serve with lime wedges.

CHEF'S TIP

You could also use shellfish, squid or cubes of fish with this recipe.

Stir-fried mussels & clams

with chilli jam

serves 4
••••

preparation
15 minutes

cooking
6 minutes

This is a very simple dish to prepare, consisting of only a few ingredients, and the flavours are delicious. It is the sort of dish that encourages you to roll up your sleeves and get stuck in. You could use clams or mussels or a combination of the two.

fresh

750 g mussels, cleaned and beards removed (or clams or other seafood if preferred)

300 g clams, cleaned

3 cm piece of ginger, peeled and thinly sliced

2 lemongrass stems, tough outer leaves removed and stems finely chopped

4 tablespoons Fresh chilli jam (see page 239)

1 small bunch of Thai basil, leaves picked and washed

juice of 2 limes

spices

freshly ground black pepper

pantry/larder

2 tablespoons vegetable oil

salt

1. Prepare the mussels and clams (see below).

2. Heat a heavy-based pan or wok over medium–high heat. Add the oil and fry half the ginger and lemongrass for 1–2 minutes until fragrant and aromatic. Add the Fresh chilli jam and the mussels and clams and cook over a high heat, stirring to coat with the jam.

3. Add 100 ml of water, cover with a lid and cook over high heat, shaking the pan every now and again, for 2 minutes. Remove the lid and stir from the bottom. Replace the lid and cook for another 2 minutes until all the mussels and clams have opened.

4. Add half the basil and the lime juice and season with plenty of black pepper. Taste the juice and adjust the seasoning if needed: it may need a little salt. Mix together and serve in prepared bowls with all the juice poured over the top. Garnish with the remaining basil, lemongrass and ginger.

> ### * how to *
> ## PREPARE SHELLFISH
>
>
>
> * *Wash the mussels (or other shellfish) in plenty of cold running water. Remove any dirt or barnacles with an old knife.*
>
> * *Debeard the mussels and then wash until the water is completely clear.*
>
> * *Discard any that do not close when they are tapped firmly on the benchtop, as they are dead and shouldn't be cooked, and also discard any that smell.*

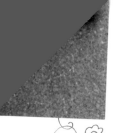

serves 4-6

● ● ● ─ ● ● ● ● ●

preparation
15 minutes

marinating
10 minutes

cooking
10 minutes

fresh

5 red chillies, seeded and finely chopped

2 garlic cloves, finely chopped

4 cm piece of ginger, peeled and finely chopped

4 coriander sprigs, leaves picked and stems finely chopped

juice of 3 limes

1 large firm white-fleshed fish (round or flat: sea bream or ocean perch is perfect)

4 lemongrass stems, tough outer leaves removed and stems finely chopped

spices

½ teaspoon freshly ground white pepper

pantry/larder

salt

2 tablespoons fish sauce

1 teaspoon caster sugar

Grilled fish
with chilli, garlic & ginger

The cuisine of Southern Thailand is famous for its great seafood dishes and its almost compulsory use of fiery red chillies, but you can tone down the chilli content of this dish if you prefer.

1. Grind the chopped red chillies and garlic using a mortar and pestle. Add a little salt to work as an abrasive and help break down the fibrous spices. Add the ginger and coriander stems and work into a paste. Add 1 tablespoon of the fish sauce, the juice of one of the limes and a splash of water.

2. Cut four diagonal slashes on each side of the fish, cutting right down to the bone. Rub the chilli paste into the slashes on both sides and make sure the fish is well covered. Set aside to marinate for 5–10 minutes in the refrigerator while you preheat the grill and make the dressing.

3. Preheat a grill, barbecue or griddle pan on high heat. Meanwhile, put the lemongrass in a mortar and pestle with a pinch of salt and the sugar and pound to a rough paste. Continue to pound and add the white pepper and coriander leaves until you have a semismooth paste. Add the remaining fish sauce and lime juice and mix until well blended. Add 50 ml of water and combine. Set aside until ready to serve.

4. If using a chargrill or barbecue, you will need a thin metal rack, such as a cake rack. If using an overhead grill, you will need a flat baking tray lined with foil. Arrange the fish for either style of cooking. Grill the fish for about 4–5 minutes on each side, depending on the weight. Be careful not to tear the skin when you turn it over.

5. When the fish is cooked, arrange it on a large platter and splash the lemongrass and pepper dressing over the top.

The slashes that have been cut in the fish allow the spice paste to permeate the flesh and the direct heat to penetrate right to the bone, caramelising the fish.

CHEF'S TIP

Curries & soups

chapter 5

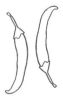

Coconut fish curry

serves 4-6
●●●●–●●●●●

preparation
15 minutes

cooking
25 minutes

You can use any combination of fish or shellfish for this dish, but make sure the end result always has a balance of hot, sweet, salt and sour.

fresh

5 garlic cloves

3 small red onions, chopped

4 cm piece of ginger, peeled

2 lemongrass stems, tough outer leaves removed and stems chopped

grated zest of 1 lime

3 kaffir lime leaves

juice of 2 limes

300 g firm white-fleshed fish (such as cod or ling), cut into 2 cm cubes

200 g large raw prawns, peeled and deveined

200 g cooked crabmeat (or scored squid or another fish or shellfish of your choice)

3 coriander sprigs, leaves picked

3 mint sprigs, leaves picked

spices

6 dried red chillies, cut in half and soaked in warm water until softened

1 teaspoon ground turmeric

freshly ground black pepper

pantry/larder

1 teaspoon salt

1 tablespoon vegetable oil

2 teaspoons prawn paste (see page 18)

660 ml coconut cream

1 tablespoon fish sauce

1 tablespoon tamarind pulp

1. Put the softened chillies in a food processor or blender with the garlic, red onions, ginger, lemongrass, lime zest and salt. Purée to a smooth paste.

2. Heat a heavy-based frying pan over medium heat and add a little oil. Fry the prawn paste for 2 minutes until fragrant and aromatic, then add the blended ingredients.

3. Add the turmeric and kaffir lime leaves and cook the paste slowly for about 10 minutes. Add the coconut cream and cook until it has reduced by a third. Taste to check the balance of flavours and adjust if needed.

4. Add the lime juice, fish sauce and tamarind pulp. Season the fish with salt and black pepper and add it to the simmering curry. Simmer gently for 2 minutes.

5. Add the prawns and cook for 1 minute, then add the crabmeat. Stir the fish so that it is all coated in the sauce, but do not let it boil, as the fish will break up.

6. Tear the coriander and mint leaves into the sauce. Taste one more time and add more lime or fish sauce if necessary. Serve with rice or noodles.

Thai green curry
with prawns

serves 4-6
●●●–●●●●●

preparation
10 minutes

cooking
10 minutes

The best way to make a really good curry is to make a big batch of curry paste, then you can freeze the leftover paste in small containers so that you can pull out a stunning curry whenever you want.

fresh

1 portion of Green curry paste (see page 224)

2 lemongrass stems, tough outer leaves removed and stems thinly sliced

150 g trimmed green beans (snow peas or asparagus can also be used)

juice of 2 limes

juice of 1 orange

500 g large raw prawns, peeled and deveined

3 coriander sprigs, leaves picked

2 Thai basil sprigs, leaves picked

2 long green chillies, seeded and finely chopped

3 spring onions, finely chopped

pantry/larder

300 ml coconut cream

1 tablespoon tamarind pulp

1 tablespoon fish sauce

1. Heat the curry paste in a saucepan over medium heat until just steaming. Add half the coconut cream and bring to the boil (you can always add more cream later if needed).

2. Add half the lemongrass and simmer gently over a low heat, stirring occasionally to stop it from sticking. Thin the paste, if necessary, with a little water.

3. Add the green beans and simmer for 2 minutes. Reduce the sauce by continuing to simmer for another 3 minutes.

4. Add the tamarind pulp, the juice of one of the limes, the orange juice and fish sauce and stir together. Add the prawns and continue simmering.

5. Coarsely chop the herbs and stir about a third into the simmering sauce. Taste the sauce to check the balance of flavours and adjust if needed to get a balance of hot, sour, salty and sweet. Garnish the finished curry with the remaining lemongrass and herbs and the green chillies and spring onions. Serve with rice or noodles.

serves 4-6
●●●–●●●●●

preparation
5 minutes

cooking
10 minutes

Red curry
with chicken

This is one of my favourite curries as it has everything in one mouthful: roasted meat, spices, heat, herbs such as Thai basil, then the sourness of pineapple and tamarind. It is a delicious combination of flavours.

fresh

1 garlic clove, finely chopped

1 portion of Red curry paste (see page 223)

3 grilled skinless and boneless chicken breasts

½ fresh pineapple, peeled and cut into chunks

6 cherry tomatoes, halved

4 Thai basil sprigs (or use regular basil), leaves picked

1 large red chilli, seeded and finely chopped, to serve

4 cm piece of ginger, peeled and thinly sliced into matchsticks, to serve

pantry/larder

2 tablespoons vegetable oil

250 ml coconut cream

1 tablespoon fish sauce

1 teaspoon grated palm sugar

1. Heat the oil in a heavy-based pan over medium–high heat. Fry the garlic until golden brown, then stir in the curry paste and heat through. Add the coconut cream, stirring constantly, and bring to the boil.

2. Turn down the heat. Add the fish sauce and palm sugar and simmer for 5 minutes.

3. Add the grilled chicken and coat in the sauce. Add the pineapple and tomatoes and stir in the Thai basil. Garnish with chopped red chilli and ginger and serve with rice or noodles.

· 6 ways with ·
COCONUT

 Steamed mussels & prawns

Heat a splash of oil, add 500 g of cleaned mussels and 2 tablespoons of red curry paste.

Add 5 kaffir lime leaves and 2 chopped lemongrass stems.

Stir in 200 ml of coconut cream.

Bring to the boil with 3 tablespoons of fish sauce and the juice of 1 lemon.

Add 250 g of peeled raw prawns. Cover and cook for 2 minutes until the prawns are cooked and the mussels have opened.

Tear a handful of coriander leaves into the mussels and serve with lime wedges.

 Set coconut cream

Simmer 200 ml of double cream, ¼ teaspoon of agar-agar powder and 40 g of caster sugar in a saucepan. Stir to dissolve the sugar.

Take off the heat and stir in 100 ml of coconut cream.

Pour into 480 ml ramekins and transfer to the refrigerator for 2 hours to set.

Dry-fry 200 g of desiccated coconut in a frying pan until golden.

Add 1 teaspoon of ground cinnamon, ½ teaspoon of ground nutmeg and ¼ teaspoon of ground cardamom and cook until fragrant.

Zest 1 lemon and 1 orange and add to the coconut.

Turn out the set puddings, scatter the coconut over the top and drizzle with runny honey.

 Turmeric & coconut fried fish

Mix together a peeled, grated 4 cm piece of ginger, 2 chopped red chillies, 50 g of rice flour, 100 ml of coconut cream, 2 eggs, 1 teaspoon of ground turmeric, 2 chopped spring onions, a pinch of salt and 2 tablespoons of toasted flaked coconut.

Dust 300 g of firm white fish fillets with rice flour so that they are coated.

Heat some vegetable oil for deep frying in a wok or frying pan. Dip the floured fish into the turmeric batter and shake off any excess.

Fry the fish in small batches for 3–4 minutes until the batter is golden and the fish is cooked. Serve with Green chilli nahm jim (see page 237).

 Creamy pumpkin soup

Finely chop 2 garlic cloves, 2 coriander roots and 2 green chillies and fry in a little oil. Add ½ teaspoon of ground nutmeg and ¼ teaspoon of ground cloves.

Dice 300 g of butternut squash or pumpkin into fine cubes, coat in the spices and season with salt and pepper.

Add 600 ml of coconut milk and simmer until the pumpkin is soft. Add the juice of 2 limes and 2 tablespoons of fish sauce.

Dry-fry 3 tablespoons of desiccated coconut in a frying pan until golden.

Pour the soup into bowls and garnish with the toasted coconut and coriander leaves.

 Thai rice salad

Put 500 g of room temperature cooked jasmine rice in a large bowl.

Dry-fry 3 tablespoons of desiccated coconut in a frying pan until golden brown. Add the coconut to the rice, along with 50 g of bean sprouts, 2 chopped spring onions and 1 diced cucumber.

Add the leaves from 3 sprigs of mint and basil.

Mix in 200 g of cold roast chicken or pork, ripped into shreds.

Crush 2 chopped red chillies and 1 tablespoon of ginger with a pinch of salt using a mortar and pestle until smooth. Add 60 ml of coconut cream, the juice of 1 lime and 2 tablespoons of fish sauce.

Mix together the rice and dressing and serve with lime wedges and Hot and sour red chilli dressing (see page 234).

 Green herb barbecue chicken

Crush 3 coriander roots, 1 tablespoon of grated ginger, 2 garlic cloves with a little salt using a mortar and pestle.

Finely chop 4 coriander sprigs and pound them until smooth.

Combine the coriander and ginger paste with 1 teaspoon of the ground coriander, a large pinch of crushed chilli, 75 ml of coconut cream and 2 tablespoons of fish sauce.

Marinate 8 chicken drumsticks in the coconut mixture for 1 hour.

Make a large foil parcel with the chicken and tightly seal the edges.

Grill the chicken parcel on a hot barbecue for about 15 minutes, turning regularly to avoid burning. When cooked, add the juice of 1 lime and scatter with some coriander leaves.

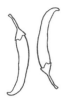

Hot & sour orange curry
with grilled salmon

The fillets of salmon in this vibrant curry are chargrilled rare first to give them a great texture and flavour, then finished off in the curry sauce.

serves 4–6
●●●–●●●●

preparation
5 minutes

cooking
10 minutes

fresh

500 g salmon fillets

1 portion of Hot and sour orange curry paste (see page 227)

100 g green beans, topped and tailed

100 g asparagus, cut into 3 cm lengths

1 red chilli, seeded

2 lemongrass stems, tough outer leaves removed and stems finely chopped

3 kaffir lime leaves, thick stems removed and shredded

½ small bunch of coriander, leaves picked

juice of 2 limes

spices

freshly ground black pepper

pantry/larder

salt

1 tablespoon fish sauce

1. Preheat a griddle pan over high heat. Season the salmon with salt and black pepper and grill the fillets for 2 minutes on each side to create griddle marks on the fish: you are not cooking the fish all the way through, just searing it on the outside.

2. Heat the curry paste in a deep-sided frying pan over medium heat. Turn down the heat, add the grilled fish and poach gently for about 2 minutes, then add the green beans and asparagus and cook for another 3 minutes.

3. Add half the chilli, lemongrass and kaffir lime leaves to the pan and stir through. Serve the curry garnished with the remaining chilli, lemongrass and lime leaves and plenty of coriander. Stir the lime juice and the fish sauce through to balance the flavours. Serve with rice.

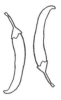

Massaman curry
with spiced braised beef

serves 4-6
•••—•••••

preparation
15 minutes

cooking
3½ hours

For this curry you will need to slow cook some beef. Cuts of meat that will work well are shin of beef, braising steak, chuck steak or topside. Alternatively, you could use an osso bucco-style cut. Lamb shoulder, lamb shanks or chicken also work well.

fresh
1 kg braising steak

1 onion, coarsely chopped

2 garlic cloves

1 carrot, chopped

1 celery stalk, chopped

3 bay leaves

4 cm piece of ginger, peeled and sliced

½ long red chilli, seeded

1 portion of Massaman curry paste with toasted peanuts (see page 228)

3 potatoes, peeled and cut into 2 cm chunks

juice of 1 lime

3 coriander sprigs, to garnish

steamed rice, to serve (optional)

spices
3 cinnamon sticks

4 star anise

freshly ground black pepper

pantry/larder
vegetable oil, for frying

salt

300 ml coconut cream

1 tablespoon fish sauce

1. Preheat the oven 150°C.

2. Heat a little vegetable oil in a heavy-based ovenproof pan and brown the steak on all sides. Add the onion, garlic, carrot, celery, bay leaves, ginger and chilli and continue to cook until browned. Add the dried spices and season with salt and black pepper. Cover the meat with water and bring to the boil. Cover with a lid and cook in the oven for at least 3 hours until meltingly soft. Remove from the heat and set aside.

3. When ready to make the curry, heat the coconut cream with 3 tablespoons of the beef braising juices. Add the curry paste and bring to the boil, stirring regularly to avoid the paste sticking. Add the potatoes and cook in the coconut cream for 10 minutes or until softened.

4. Cut the braised beef into six pieces. When the potatoes are three-quarters cooked, add the beef to the curry. Don't break up the beef any more as it will do that naturally as it cooks in the sauce. Add another 3 tablespoons of the braising liquid.

5. Taste to check the balance of flavours and adjust if needed: it should taste sweet, sour and salty, with a strong roasted spice base.

6. Add the fish sauce and lime juice to bring the flavours into balance and highlight all the toasted spices. Garnish with coriander and serve with steamed rice if desired.

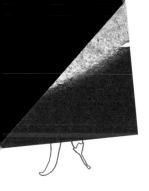

Geng gari curry
with roast chicken

A geng gari is a delicious curry with a base of ground toasted spices, which add a delicious earthy foundation to the curry. This would work really well as a vegetarian curry with roasted sweet potato and butternut squash.

serves 4-6
● ● ● ● – ● ● ● ● ●

preparation
10 minutes

cooking
15 minutes

fresh

250 g chicken, cut into pieces

1 portion of Geng gari paste (see page 226)

100 g baby corn

juice of 2 limes

20 Thai basil leaves, coarsely chopped

2 cm piece of ginger, peeled and thinly sliced into matchsticks

3 spring onions, thinly sliced, to garnish

spices

1 teaspoon coriander seeds

1 teaspoon cumin seeds

freshly ground black pepper

pantry/larder

salt

1 tablespoon tamarind pulp

2 tablespoons light soy sauce

vegetable oil, for cooking

1. Coarsely crush the coriander and cumin seeds using a mortar and pestle. Season the chicken with salt, black pepper and the crushed spices and drizzle with a little vegetable oil.

2. Pan-fry or grill the chicken over medium–high heat for about 10 minutes until golden brown and caramelised on all sides. To check that the chicken is cooked all the way through, cut into the meat with the point of a sharp knife; the meat should be white and the juices should be clear and not pink.

3. Heat the curry paste in a frying pan over medium heat and add the baby corn. Add the lime juice, tamarind and light soy sauce along with half the Thai basil and the ginger.

4. Taste the curry paste to check the balance of flavours and adjust if needed: it should be hot, sour and salty.

5. Garnish with spring onions and the remaining Thai basil. Serve as an accompaniment to other dishes, such as crisp salads, rice dishes or vegetables.

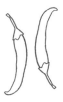

Tom yum

hot & sour soup with roast shallots, chicken & basil

serves 4-6
●●●—●●●●●

preparation
15 minutes

cooking
35 minutes

The fine-tuning of the dish can be left to the individual by having a plate on the table containing chilli, herbs, lime wedges and light soy or fish sauce. This enables each guest to create a flavour balance that suits their palate.

fresh

2 lemongrass stems, tough outer leaves removed and stems chopped

4 cm piece of ginger, peeled and chopped

5 garlic cloves, chopped

2 red chillies, seeded and coarsely chopped

4 coriander roots, washed and coarsely chopped

500 ml fresh chicken stock (you can buy fresh stock from your butcher or supermarket)

3 kaffir lime leaves, chopped

6 shallots, thinly sliced

juice of 3 limes, plus extra lime wedges to serve

2 grilled chicken breasts, cut into slices

2 spring onions, thinly sliced

3 coriander sprigs, leaves picked and coarsely chopped

2 Thai basil sprigs (or regular basil), coarsely chopped

pantry/larder

vegetable oil, for cooking

2 tablespoons tamarind pulp

4 tablespoons fish sauce

2 teaspoons grated palm sugar

1. Heat 1 tablespoon of oil in a heavy-based frying pan over medium heat. Add the lemongrass, ginger, garlic, chillies and coriander roots and fry for about 3 minutes until golden brown. Add the stock, kaffir lime leaves, tamarind pulp and 2 tablespoons of the fish sauce and simmer for 20 minutes.

2. Meanwhile, in a separate frying pan, cook the shallots in a little oil with the grated palm sugar for 10–12 minutes.

3. Strain the stock through a sieve into a bowl and discard the flavouring ingredients. Pour the stock back into the pan and bring the liquid to the boil. Add the lime juice and the remaining fish sauce. Taste to check the balance of flavours and adjust if needed: it should have an underlying sweetness from the stock and caramelised vegetables.

4. When the soup is ready, place the sliced chicken and caramelised shallots in the bottom of each serving bowl. Add the spring onions, chopped coriander and Thai basil leaves and pour the soup over the ingredients in the bowl. Add a squeeze of lime to each bowl and serve.

Roast duck soup
with lime, chilli & basil

serves 4-6
●●●●—●●●●●

preparation
10 minutes

cooking
7 minutes

This is a delicious, simple soup with lots of lime juice, hot chillies and zingy Thai basil. It is so refreshing and could be made with either roast chicken or roast duck.

fresh

2 garlic cloves, finely chopped

3 small bird's eye chillies, bruised

3 lemongrass stems, bruised and cut into quarters

1.5 litres fresh chicken stock (you can buy fresh stock from your butcher or supermarket)

½ roast duck (from a Chinese restaurant), meat shredded and skin discarded

juice of 3 limes

4 Thai basil sprigs (or regular basil), leaves picked and coarsely chopped

pantry/larder

1 teaspoon grated palm sugar

2 tablespoons fish sauce

salt

1. Put the garlic, bruised chillies, palm sugar and bruised lemongrass in a saucepan. Add the chicken stock and bring to the boil. Reduce the heat and simmer for 5 minutes. Use a slotted spoon to remove the lemongrass pieces from the stock and discard.

2. Add the duck, fish sauce and lime juice, stir together and taste to check the balance of flavours: it may need a little salt. Add the chopped Thai basil leaves and taste again before serving.

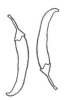

Tom kha gai
chicken & coconut milk soup

serves 4-6
● ● ● ● — ● ● ● ● ●

preparation
10 minutes

cooking
15 minutes

This is a deliciously fragrant soup. It's aromatic and mild and not too spicy and is served alongside hotter dishes so the heat of the meal is tempered.

fresh

5 cm piece of galangal or ginger, peeled, bruised with the back of a knife and cut into thick slices

4 lemongrass stems, bruised with the back of knife and cut into 4–5 pieces

500 g boneless chicken breast fillet, cut into 2 cm thick slices

4 small bird's eye chillies, bruised with the back of knife

5 kaffir lime leaves, torn

juice of 2 limes

4 coriander sprigs, leaves picked and torn

lime wedges, to serve (optional)

pantry/larder

1.25 litres coconut milk

125 ml coconut cream

3 tablespoons fish sauce

1. Put the galangal and lemongrass in a large saucepan and add the thin coconut milk. Bring slowly to the boil, stirring regularly. Simmer gently for 5 minutes, then add the chicken and simmer for another 5 minutes until the chicken is cooked.

2. Add the thick coconut cream, fish sauce, chillies, kaffir lime leaves and lime juice and bring almost to the boil, stirring, then remove from the heat. Transfer to warmed bowls and garnish with torn coriander leaves. Serve with lime wedges, if using.

Rice, noodles & sides

chapter 6

Pad thai fried noodles

This is probably one of the most famous dishes in and out of Thailand, and is not too challenging on the palate for anyone unfamiliar with Thai cuisine.

serves 4-6

● ● ● ● — ● ● ● ● ●

preparation
10 minutes

cooking
8 minutes

fresh

100 g silken tofu, cut into small cubes

2 garlic cloves, finely chopped

250 g skinless and boneless chicken breast, cut into thin strips

200 g raw prawns, peeled, deveined and halved lengthways

1 egg

juice of ½ lemon

100 g bean sprouts, washed and trimmed

1 fresh red chilli, seeded and finely chopped

4 spring onions, finely chopped

3 coriander sprigs, leaves picked

lemon wedges, to serve

spices

¼ teaspoon dried chilli flakes

pantry/larder

2 tablespoons vegetable oil

175 g sen lek noodles (see page 17), soaked in warm water for 20 minutes until soft, then drained

2 tablespoons fish sauce

2 tablespoons blanched skinless peanuts, toasted then crushed

1. Heat the oil in a wok over medium heat and fry the tofu for about 3 minutes until golden brown. Add the garlic and cook for 30 seconds. Add the chicken and stir-fry for 1 minute. After a minute, add the prawns and stir well.

2. Break in the egg and stir quickly, cooking for a couple of seconds. Add the soaked noodles and stir well.

3. Mix in the lemon juice, fish sauce and dried chilli flakes. Add half the beansprouts, half the fresh chilli and half the spring onions. Keep stir-frying for about 3 minutes until the noodles are cooked through.

4. Turn the noodles out onto a serving plate and garnish with the remaining fresh chilli, spring onions, beansprouts and the coriander leaves. Serve with lemon wedges and scatter the peanuts over.

serves 4-6

● ● ● ● – ● ● ● ● ● ●

preparation
10 minutes

cooking
7–8 minutes

Fried rice
with prawns, squid & crab

This is a delicious Thai rice dish. I use prawns, squid and crab, but you could use any fish or shellfish that you want. You can vary the heat content and serve it with a spicy dipping sauce or some dried red chillies.

fresh

1 brown onion, finely chopped

3 garlic cloves, finely chopped

2 red chillies, seeded and finely chopped

250 g raw prawns, peeled, deveined and halved lengthways

200 g squid, cleaned and underside scored in a diamond pattern (see page 116)

2 eggs, beaten

250 g cooked jasmine or fragrant rice

200 g cooked crabmeat, picked (available from a good fishmonger)

juice of 2 limes

3 coriander sprigs, leaves picked and coarsely chopped

2 spring onions, finely chopped

2 basil sprigs, leaves picked

sliced cucumber, to serve

Green chilli nahm jim dressing (see page 237), to serve (optional)

spices

freshly ground black pepper

pantry/larder

2 tablespoons vegetable oil

3 tablespoons fish sauce

1. Heat the vegetable oil in a wok over medium heat and fry the onion for 1–2 minutes until softened. Add the garlic and chillies and fry for another minute until fragrant and aromatic.

2. Add the prawns, stir-fry briskly for 1 minute, then add the scored squid and stir-fry for another minute. Add the beaten eggs, cooking it on the upper edges of the pan so that you get a thin omelette.

3. Splash in the fish sauce, then add the cooked rice and crabmeat and continue to stir-fry for 3 minutes. Season with black pepper and lime juice.

4. Add the coriander and spring onions and tear in the basil leaves, then quickly transfer to a large serving dish. Serve with cucumber slices and Green chilli nahm jim dressing (if using).

serves 4-6

● ● ● ● – ● ● ● ● ●

preparation
5 minutes

cooking
3 minutes

Pad ki mow
spicy beef noodles with kaffir lime leaves

You can use any meat and vary the ingredients and also the heat content of the dish to suit your taste. The noodles will double in weight when they are soaked.

fresh

2 garlic cloves, finely chopped

2 fresh red chillies, seeded and finely chopped

400 g beef rump, cut into thin strips

4 kaffir lime leaves, shredded

2 Thai basil sprigs (or regular basil), leaves picked

3 coriander sprigs, leaves picked and torn, to serve

lime wedges, to serve

spices

¼ teaspoon dried chilli flakes

½ teaspoon five-spice powder

pantry/larder

2 tablespoons vegetable oil

2 tablespoons fish sauce

½ teaspoon grated palm sugar

125 g sen yai noodles (see page 17), soaked in warm water for 20 minutes until soft, then drained

1. Heat the oil in a wok over medium heat. Add the garlic and fry for 1 minute or until golden. Add the chillies and stir-fry for 10 seconds, then add the beef and stir-fry for about 20 seconds to seal the meat.

2. Add the fish sauce, palm sugar, shredded kaffir lime leaves, half the basil leaves and the dried chilli and five-spice, stir-frying all the time.

3. Add the soaked and drained noodles and stir well. Keep stir-frying for about 1 minute, then taste the noodles to check that they are cooked.

4. Turn out the noodles onto a serving plate and garnish with torn coriander leaves, the remaining Thai basil and lime wedges.

Hakka-style fried noodles
with pork & Thai basil

serves 4
••••

preparation
10 minutes

cooking
4 minutes

These noodles are so quick and deliciously juicy, plus the Thai basil gives it a fantastic liquorice–aniseed taste. You could use any combination of meat and vegetables.

fresh

300 g pork fillet, cut into thin slices

2 long red chillies, seeded and finely chopped

4 cm piece of ginger, peeled and finely grated

800 g fresh egg noodles

250 ml fresh chicken stock (you can buy fresh stock from your butcher or supermarket)

½ bunch of garlic chives, cut into 1 cm lengths (available from Asian grocery stores, but if unavailable, use normal chives)

200 g bean sprouts, washed and trimmed

3 Thai basil sprigs (or regular basil), leaves picked

Hot and sour red chilli dressing (see page 234), to serve

spices

½ teaspoon ground white pepper

pantry/larder

2 tablespoons vegetable oil

3 tablespoons light soy sauce

1½ tablespoons dark soy sauce

1. Heat the oil in a wok over medium heat and stir-fry the pork and red chillies for 1 minute. Add the ginger, noodles and half the stock, a little at a time, stirring to combine. Cover with a lid, turn the heat down and simmer for 1 minute.

2. Add the light and dark soy sauce and stir-fry for 1 minute. Add a little extra stock if the noodles are sticking.

3. Season with white pepper, add the garlic chives and beansprouts, stirring all the time. Taste the noodles to check for the balance of flavours and adjust if needed. Add the Thai basil and serve with the Hot and sour red chilli dressing.

GINGER & GARLIC

 Ginger, mint & prawn salad

Pound 1 tablespoon of ginger peelings using a mortar and pestle for 2 minutes until it is a smooth pulp. Remove with a spoon.

Add 20 mint leaves, ½ teaspoon of caster sugar and ½ teaspoon of salt to the mortar and pestle and pound to a smooth green paste.

Juice 2 limes into the paste and add 2 chopped red chillies.

Squeeze the ginger pulp in the palm of your hand into the mortar and pestle, wringing out all the fresh juice.

Mix everything together and then pour it over 200 g of cooked prawns. Garnish with the leaves picked from 3 sprigs of coriander.

 Grilled fish with garlic, pepper & chilli dressing

Crush 2 garlic cloves with a little salt to a paste using a mortar and pestle.

Chop 3 seeded green chillies and 2 coriander roots and mix with the garlic paste, along with the juice of 2 lemons and 2 tablespoons of fish sauce.

Rub half this mixture onto 4 fish fillets (such as sardines or red mullet). Preheat the grill or barbecue to hot and cook the fish for 3 minutes on each side.

Stir 1 teaspoon of grated palm sugar or soft brown sugar into the remaining dressing along with ½ teaspoon of crushed white pepper.

Serve the fish with the dressing poured over the top.

❸ Crisp cucumber & chicken salad with ginger

Pound 1 garlic clove, 1 seeded and chopped red chilli, ½ teaspoon of salt and ½ teaspoon of caster sugar using a mortar and pestle until smooth. Add the juice of 1 orange and 2 limes.

Peel and grate a 4 cm piece of ginger, slice 3 spring onions, seed 1 cucumber and cut into 4 cm batons.

Shred the meat from half a roast chicken and mix with the cucumber.

Pick the leaves from 3 sprigs of coriander and finely shred them.

Combine all the ingredients together for the salad and dressing and pour it over the chicken and cucumber.

 Peppered chicken with chilli & garlic dressing

Cut 300 g of boneless, skinless chicken breast into 3 cm pieces. Add 2 tablespoons of light soy sauce, ½ tablespoon of dark soy sauce and 2 teaspoons of ground black pepper.

Pound 2 garlic cloves and 2 seeded and chopped red chillies with a pinch of salt using a mortar and pestle until smooth. Add the leaves from 4 sprigs of coriander and continue to pound to a paste.

Preheat the grill to hot. Skewer the chicken and grill it slowly, for about 8 minutes, turning frequently to caramelise on all sides.

Add the juice of 2 limes and 5 tablespoons of warm water to the garlic paste and serve the sauce with the chicken skewers.

 Garlic grilled pork chops

Crush 2 garlic cloves, 1 teaspoon of coriander seeds, 1 teaspoon of fennel seeds, 4 star anise, a pinch of salt and a pinch of dried chilli flakes, using a mortar and pestle.

Rub the crushed mixture into 4 pork chops.

Preheat the grill to hot and grill the pork chops for 6 minutes on one side.

Turn the pork chops over and grill for 2 minutes, then remove from the heat and rest for about 2 minutes before serving.

Mix together a dressing of 1 tablespoon of grated ginger, the juice of 2 limes, ¼ teaspoon of crushed white pepper and 1 tablespoon of fish sauce and pour this over the chops.

 Grilled beef with ginger & coconut

Dry-fry 50 g of flaked coconut, 1 tablespoon of crushed coriander seeds, a 4 cm piece of peeled and grated ginger and 1 seeded and chopped red chilli over medium heat in a frying pan.

Cook slowly until the coconut and coriander are golden, toasted and fragrant.

Grill 400 g beef sirloin or rump until medium–rare and then rest.

Tear the leaves from 3 sprigs each of coriander and mint and add to the coconut.

Slice the beef thinly and add the juice of 1 lime and 1 tablespoon of fish sauce.

Scatter with the coconut mint garnish.

Braised chicken
with rice, turmeric & spices

serves 4–6
●●●–●●●●●

preparation
15 minutes

cooking
15–18 minutes

This dish is essentially a pilaf where the chicken and rice are cooked together. It is a very easy dish to make and perfect for the whole family.

fresh

500 g skinless, boneless chicken thighs, cut into 3 cm cubes

2 garlic cloves, chopped

2 red chillies, seeded and finely chopped

3 coriander roots, chopped

4 cm piece of ginger, peeled and finely grated

200 ml fresh chicken stock

3 spring onions, finely chopped

juice of 2 limes

2 mint sprigs, leaves picked

3 coriander sprigs, leaves picked

spices

1 teaspoon ground cinnamon

1 teaspoon ground coriander

1 teaspoon ground turmeric

½ teaspoon ground cardamom

pantry/larder

2 tablespoons vegetable oil

100 g basmati rice

2 tablespoons light soy sauce

1. Heat the vegetable oil in a heavy-based frying pan over medium heat. Add the chicken and brown for 4–5 minutes until golden brown. Add the garlic, chillies, coriander roots and ginger and cook for about 1 minute until fragrant. Add the dried spices and cook for another minute. Be careful that they do not scorch.

2. Add the rice and stir together so that the spices start to coat the rice. Add the chicken stock and the soy sauce and cover with a lid. Simmer gently for 10–12 minutes until the rice is cooked and all the liquid has been absorbed.

3. Add the spring onions and lime juice and tear in the mint and coriander leaves. Mix together and serve.

CHEF'S TIP

You could also make this with fish or seafood, but you would need to add the pieces of fish halfway through the cooking process as it won't take as long to cook.

Thai fried rice

serves 4-6

●●●–●●●●●

preparation
10 minutes

cooking
10 minutes

This Thai staple is a great way of using up delicious leftovers: you could use chicken satay, spice-roast pork, prawns, grilled fish or vegetables.

fresh

1 brown onion, finely chopped

3 garlic cloves, finely chopped

2 red chillies, seeded and finely chopped

2 skinless and boneless chicken breasts, sliced into 5 mm slices

250 g raw prawns, peeled, cleaned and halved lengthways

2 eggs, beaten

800 g cold cooked jasmine rice

juice of 2 limes

3 coriander sprigs, leaves picked and coarsely chopped

2 spring onions, finely chopped

spices

freshly ground black pepper

pantry/larder

2 tablespoons vegetable oil

3 tablespoons fish sauce

1. Heat the vegetable oil in a wok over medium heat and fry the onion for 1–2 minutes until softened. Add the garlic and chillies and fry for another minute until fragrant and aromatic.

2. Add the sliced chicken and stir-fry briskly until the chicken starts to change colour, then add the raw prawns. Stir-fry briskly for 2 minutes, then add the beaten egg, cooking it on the upper edges of the pan so that you are getting a thin omelette.

3. Splash in the fish sauce, then add the rice and continue to stir-fry for 3 minutes. Season with black pepper and lime juice.

4. Add the coriander and spring onions, then quickly transfer to a large serving dish.

CHEF'S TIP Serve with Nahm jim dressing (see pages 236–237), Hot and sour red chilli dressing (see page 234) or Peanut dipping sauce (see page 242).

Braised mushrooms
with ginger & chilli

serves 4
• • • •

preparation
10 minutes

cooking
8–10 minutes

Mushrooms with ginger are really delicious. Serve this with some roasted meat, such as the Slow roast pork shoulder (see page 104). You can use a combination of different cultivated and wild mushrooms in this dish if preferred.

fresh

3 coriander roots, cleaned and finely chopped

1 red chilli, seeded and finely chopped

2 garlic cloves, finely chopped

4 cm piece of ginger, peeled and finely grated

400 g oyster mushrooms, torn

100 g asparagus, cut into 4 cm lengths

juice of 1 lime

2 coriander sprigs, leaves picked and coarsely torn

spices

½ teaspoon ground cinnamon

½ teaspoon five-spice powder

½ teaspoon ground coriander

freshly ground black pepper

pantry/larder

2 tablespoons vegetable oil

salt

100 ml rice wine

1 tablespoon light soy sauce

1 tablespoon toasted sesame seeds

1. Combine the coriander roots, red chilli, garlic and ginger and mix together.

2. Heat the oil in a heavy-based pan over medium–high heat and fry the coriander root mixture until fragrant and aromatic.

3. Add the torn mushrooms and cook over high heat for about 3–4 minutes until the mushrooms start to smell nutty and are beginning to caramelise and turn golden brown.

4. Add the dried spices and season well with salt and black pepper. Add the rice wine, soy sauce and asparagus and cover with a lid. Simmer for about 4 minutes until all the liquid has been absorbed.

5. Add the lime juice, coriander and toasted sesame seeds. Mix together and taste.

serves 4
●●●●

preparation
5 minutes

cooking
1 minute

Stir-fried spinach
with garlic & black pepper

When cooking in a wok you get an excellent smoky taste to the greens. Water spinach is a Thai variety that has dark green blade-shaped leaves and a hollow stem and it stir-fries in seconds. If not available, use baby spinach or a combination of spinach and other greens such as silverbeet or broccolini.

fresh

3 small garlic cloves, finely chopped

1 red chilli, seeded and finely chopped

3 cm piece of ginger, peeled and finely grated

500 g raw water spinach (or silverbeet, broccolini or a combination)

juice of 1 lemon

spices

freshly ground black pepper

pantry/larder

2 tablespoons vegetable oil

salt

2 tablespoons fish sauce

1. Heat the oil in a wok over medium heat, then add the garlic, chilli and ginger and stir-fry for about 30 seconds until golden brown.

2. Add the spinach and stir-fry quickly over high heat, so they are coated in the oil, garlic and chilli.

3. Season with salt and lots of black pepper. Add the fish sauce and lemon juice, cook for another 30 seconds and serve immediately. Serve as part of a meal with meat, fish or rice.

serves 4
••••

preparation
5 minutes

cooking
3 minutes

Stir-fried mixed greens
with oyster sauce

You can use any combination of green vegetables for this quick dish, such as broccolini, green beans or asparagus.

fresh

2 small garlic cloves, finely chopped

500 g mixed green vegetables, such as broccolini, green beans, asparagus and sugar snap peas, trimmed to equal lengths

juice of 1 lemon

3 coriander sprigs, leaves picked, to garnish

spices

a pinch of crushed dried chilli flakes

freshly ground black pepper

pantry/larder

2 tablespoons vegetable oil

2 tablespoons oyster sauce

salt

2 tablespoons sesame seeds, toasted, to garnish

1. Heat the oil in a wok over medium heat, add the garlic and stir-fry for about 30 seconds until golden brown. Add the mixed greens and a splash of water and stir-fry for about 2 minutes over high heat.

2. Add the oyster sauce and dried chilli and stir-fry for another 30 seconds so that they are coated. Season with salt and lots of black pepper. Add the lemon juice and serve immediately. Scatter with the toasted sesame seeds and coriander leaves to garnish.

Desserts
& drinks

chapter 7

Spiced banana fritters

Banana fritters are a street stall staple stacked high in newspaper cones and they make a great snack. There are lots of different variations, but I like this spicy one.

serves 4-6

●●●●–●●●●●

preparation
10 minutes

cooking
3 minutes
(per batch)

fresh

3 large unripe bananas (the skins just turning yellow)

spices

1 teaspoon ground cinnamon

½ teaspoon ground cardamom

¼ teaspoon ground nutmeg

¼ teaspoon ground cloves

pantry/larder

75 g plain flour

75 g rice flour

pinch of salt

1 tablespoon sesame seeds

225 ml coconut milk

2 tablespoons honey

light vegetable oil, for deep-frying

1. Mix both flours with the salt, ground spices and sesame seeds in a bowl. Whisk in the coconut milk until you have a smooth batter. Add the honey and whisk until you have a batter that is the consistency of double cream.

2. Slice the bananas diagonally into 3–4 large slices, then cut each slice in half lengthways so that you have strips about 1 cm thick.

3. Heat the oil for frying in a heavy-based frying pan to 200°C, or until a cube of bread dropped in browns in 15 seconds.

4. Dip the strips of banana in the batter, then shake off any excess. Deep-fry in small batches for about 3 minutes until golden brown, then drain on paper towel. Serve immediately.

serves 8
● ● ● ● ● ● ● ●

preparation
10 minutes

cooking
12 minutes

setting
40 minutes

fresh

1 packet of fresh or frozen young coconut (available from Asian grocery stores), flesh shredded and liquid reserved

grated zest of 1 orange

grated zest of 1 lemon

pantry/larder

15 g powdered agar-agar (or use gelatine – either leaves or powdered)

pinch of salt

200 g caster sugar

480 ml coconut cream

Thai citrus & young coconut jelly

This is a striking looking jelly because it has two layers; one which is clear with citrus zest, the other creamy with strips of coconut. Young coconut is available shredded and frozen in its sweet water in most Asian food stores.

1. Put 700 ml of water and 240 ml of the liquid from the packet of young coconut in a small saucepan. Stir in the agar-agar powder (or gelatine) and simmer for 10 minutes. Add the salt and sugar and stir to dissolve. If using gelatine, follow the instructions on the packet to set this amount of liquid.

2. Mix the shredded coconut flesh with the coconut cream in another saucepan. Add half the simmered sugar water and warm over low heat for about 2 minutes, but do not boil. Set aside to cool.

3. Add the orange and lemon zest to the remaining simmered sugar water and set aside to cool (the orange will begin to colour the liquid as it cools). The liquid in both saucepans will start to set as they cool.

4. Pour the coconut cream mixture into eight clean moulds, glasses or dishes, leaving a space for the clear orange jelly. Leave to set for about 20 minutes in the refrigerator.

5. Gently pour the clear orange jelly over the top of the set coconut cream layer and leave to set for 20 minutes in the refrigerator before serving. Serve with tropical Asian fruits, such as mango, papaya, watermelon or pineapple.

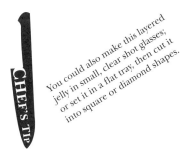

CHEF'S TIP You could also make this layered jelly in small, clear shot glasses; or set it in a flat tray, then cut it into square or diamond shapes.

Sticky rice
with mango

This is one of the most popular Thai desserts. The salt in the coconut cream is essential as it brings out the flavour of the coconut rice.

serves 6
● ● ● ● ● ●

preparation
5 minutes

cooking
10 minutes

fresh
275 g cooked and still warm Thai sticky rice (see page 248)

4 ripe mangoes

pantry/larder
250 ml coconut milk

1 tablespoon white sugar

½ teaspoon salt

2 tablespoons coconut cream

1. Put the coconut milk and sugar in a saucepan and heat gently, stirring constantly, to dissolve the sugar: be careful not to let the cream boil.

2. Add the salt and warm steamed rice and stir to combine. Set aside.

3. Cut the large cheeks off the mango as close to the centre as possible, remove the skin and cut the cheeks into 4 slices. Repeat with the other mangoes.

4. Place a mound of the sweet warm rice in the centre of a serving bowl and arrange the mango slices on top. Pour some coconut cream over the top and serve hot, warm or cold.

serves 4
••••

preparation
10–15 minutes

Mango & pineapple salad

This fruit salad is a really refreshing end to a meal, particularly on a hot day. You can also chill it slightly before serving to get the full effect of the crisp textures.

fresh

20 mint leaves

3 cm piece of ginger, peeled

juice of 1 orange

2 ripe mangoes, peeled, stoned and cut into large chunks

½ pineapple, peeled and cut into medium chunks (so they are different to the mango)

mango sorbet (or other flavour of choice), to serve

pantry/larder

1 teaspoon caster sugar

1. Put the mint leaves, sugar and ginger in a mortar and pestle and pound until you have a smooth paste. Add the orange juice and keeping working the mixture until you have a smooth dressing.

2. Put the fruit in serving bowls, pour over the dressing and gently mix together. Serve immediately with scoops of mango sorbet.

CHEF'S TIP

The key to making this zesty salad is buying good-quality ripe fruit. If this is not available, make something else and wait until you have some prime sweet fruit.

Pineapple
with caramelised chilli sauce

serves 4-6

•••• – ••••••

preparation
5 minutes

cooking
10 minutes

This is an amazing combination of flavours as the acidity of the pineapple offsets the sweet richness of the caramel.

fresh

2 red chillies, seeded and finely chopped

4 cm piece of ginger, peeled and finely grated

3 long strips of orange zest

juice of 1 lime

1 pineapple, peeled and cut into 1 cm thick slices

spices

3 cardamom pods, crushed

2 cinnamon sticks, snapped

3 star anise, broken

pantry/larder

1 tablespoon vegetable oil

50 g palm sugar, grated (or soft brown sugar)

1 tablespoon honey

1 teaspoon tamarind pulp

pinch of salt

1. Heat a splash of oil in a frying pan over medium heat and fry the chillies, ginger, all the spices and the orange zest for about 2 minutes until fragrant and aromatic. Add the palm sugar and honey and cook for 3–4 minutes until caramelised.

2. Add the tamarind pulp, salt and 80 ml of water and simmer for about 4 minutes until it is sticky and caramelised and the consistency of honey.

3. Remove from the heat and add the lime juice. Taste to check the balance of flavours and adjust if needed.

4. Arrange the pineapple on a serving platter and pour the warm spiced caramel sauce over the top to serve.

Watermelon
with lime, salt & black pepper

serves 4-6

●●●●–●●●●●

preparation
10 minutes

chilling
1 hour

This combination of flavours also works well as a deliciously refreshing drink: simply juice the watermelon, then add the other flavours just before serving.

fresh

1 small watermelon, peeled, seeded and cut into small pieces (see box below)

juice of 2 limes

spices

freshly ground black pepper

pantry/larder

salt

1. Put the watermelon in the refrigerator for at least 1 hour to chill.

2. When ready to serve, add the lime juice to the watermelon and season well with plenty of black pepper and salt — do not be shy with these two flavourings.

3. Mix together and taste to check the balance of flavours — make sure you can taste heat from the pepper, sweetness from the watermelon and salt and sourness from the lime juice — and adjust if necessary.

---

* how to *
SEED A WATERMELON

* *Use a sharp knife to cut the top and the bottom off the watermelon and remove the skin, cutting from top to bottom, so that all the skin and the white areas of flesh have been cut away.*

* *Cut each half into wedges. If you view the melon wedge from the side, it is made up of three layers: the inside or core layer is smooth with no seeds. Remove this first inside layer with a small sharp knife, then cut into bite-sized chunks.*

* *The second layer is where all the seeds are present. If you cut this into chunks every single one would have seeds in it, so use a sharp knife to remove all of this layer. This part of the melon can be used to make a delicious drink, so do not waste it. Instead, put all of this seeded section in a blender, then pass it through a sieve to get rid of all the seeds. Chill, then serve as a refreshing drink.*

Toasted coconut ice-cream topping

This delicious topping can be poured over vanilla ice cream to create a decadent dessert. It can also be scattered over tropical fruit salad, pancakes or porridge.

serves 4-6

● ● ● ● – ● ● ● ● ●

preparation
10 minutes

cooking
7 minutes

fresh

4 cm piece of ginger, peeled and finely grated

grated zest and juice of 1 orange

vanilla ice cream, to serve

spices

1 teaspoon ground cinnamon

½ teaspoon ground nutmeg

pantry/larder

200 g shredded coconut

2 tablespoons honey

1. Put the coconut and ginger in a frying pan over medium heat and dry-fry for about 3 minutes until fragrant and golden brown, keeping the pan moving so that the coconut does not scorch.

2. When the coconut is just beginning to brown, add the spices and cook for 1 minute so that they become aromatic and fragrant, but without scorching.

3. Combine the honey and 2 tablespoons of water in a saucepan over medium–high heat and bring to the boil. Add the orange zest and simmer for about 3 minutes until the honey begins to caramelise. Keep moving the caramel around the pan, taking it to a dark colour, then remove it from the heat. The caramel will continue to turn as dark as brown sugar as it cools off the heat.

4. When the caramel is dark and sticky, add the orange juice to stop the cooking.

5. Crush the spiced coconut using a mortar and pestle.

6. Scoop some vanilla ice cream into serving bowls, drizzle with the burnt honey caramel, then scatter the spiced coconut over the top to serve.

Banana & coconut pancakes

These pancakes are the perfect end to a delicious meal of satay, fishcakes and stir-fries that are all packed full of lots of flavours and fiery chillies.

serves 4-6

● ● ● — ● ● ● ● ●

preparation
15 minutes

cooking
2 minutes
(per pancake)

fresh

2 eggs, beaten

4 large ripe bananas

lemon wedges, to serve

spices

1 teaspoon ground cinnamon,
plus extra for sprinkling

pantry/larder

125 g plain flour

125 g rice flour

1 teaspoon baking powder

120 ml coconut milk

1 teaspoon soft brown sugar

pinch of salt

75 g desiccated coconut

vegetable oil, for cooking

icing sugar, for sprinkling

1. Sift both flours with the baking powder and cinnamon into a bowl. Make a well in the centre and add the beaten eggs and half the coconut milk. Mix well until you have a smooth batter, then add the remaining coconut milk.

2. Peel the bananas and put them in a bowl with the sugar and salt. Mash with a fork, then mix this into the batter. Add the desiccated coconut and mix together.

3. Heat a frying pan over medium heat, grease with a little oil and then tip out any excess oil.

4. Fry a ladleful of pancake batter at a time for about 1 minute on each side until brown. Remove from the pan and repeat until all the batter is used up.

5. Sprinkle some icing sugar on some baking paper. Turn the pancakes onto the sugar, sprinkle with a little icing sugar, a pinch of ground cinnamon and a squeeze of lemon, then fold into quarters and enjoy.

Pineapple, lime & mint crush

Serve as a refreshing drink on its own or with a dash of vodka, tequila or gin.

serves 4–6

● ● ● ● — ● ● ● ● ● ●

preparation
5 minutes

fresh

2 limes

½ pineapple, peeled and cut into chunks

3 mint sprigs, leaves picked, plus extra to garnish

4 cm piece of ginger, peeled and finely grated

1 glass full of ice cubes

mint leaves, to garnish

spices

½ teaspoon freshly ground black pepper

pantry/larder

pinch of salt

1. Use a sharp knife to cut the skin and pith from the limes, then cut the flesh into chunks.

2. Put all of the ingredients except the mint in a food processor or blender and pulse to form a frozen pineapple crush, then serve immediately garnished with mint leaves.

serves 4-6
•••• - •••••

preparation
5 minutes

cooking
12 minutes

Roasted fruits
with aromatic Thai spices

Roasted fruits with spices is the perfect dessert: it is rich and sophisticated, yet simple to make. You can use any fruits for this, depending on the season: apples, pears, quinces, peaches, nectarines and plums are all good.

fresh

4 cm piece of ginger, peeled and finely grated

grated zest and juice of 2 oranges

6 pears, peeled and quartered

20 g butter, cut into small pieces

spices

3 cardamom pods, crushed

4 star anise

3 cinnamon sticks

3 bay leaves

½ teaspoon freshly grated nutmeg

½ teaspoon allspice

¼ teaspoon freshly ground black pepper

pantry/larder

1 tablespoon grated palm sugar

2 tablespoons honey

1. Preheat the oven to 180°C.

2. Mix all of the ingredients, except the pears and the butter, together in a bowl. Add the pears and mix well so that the pear pieces are well coated.

3. Tip the pears into a roasting tin and top with the butter pieces: this will create a spiced butterscotch as it melts with the honey.

4. Bake for about 12 minutes until the fruit has caramelised, basting the fruit with the spicy caramel during cooking.

Basics

chapter 8

5 curry pastes

There are numerous types of Thai curry paste with the ingredients, quantities and flavourings varying from region to region; however, they do all follow the same basic method, so here is a selection of the most popular pastes to add to your repertoire.

Red curry paste

This is a classic red curry paste that can be used for many types of curry, from fish or prawns to roasted duck.

serves 6
•• •• ••

preparation
15 minutes

cooking
40 minutes

fresh

5 red chillies, seeded and finely chopped

2 lemongrass stems, tough outer leaves removed and stems chopped

4 cm piece of ginger, peeled and finely chopped

4 garlic cloves

6 coriander roots, washed and chopped

3 red onions, coarsely chopped

1 red capsicum, chopped

4 kaffir lime leaves

juice of 2 limes

spices

½ teaspoon ground white pepper

2 teaspoons ground turmeric

pantry/larder

2 tablespoons vegetable oil

1 teaspoon prawn paste (see page 18)

1 teaspoon salt

660 ml coconut cream

2 tablespoons fish sauce

1. Preheat the oven to 200°C.

2. Mix all of the fresh ingredients, except the kaffir lime leaves and lime juice, together in a bowl and add 1 tablespoon of the vegetable oil. Line a baking tray with baking paper and spread out the mixed fresh ingredients on the tray.

3. Spoon the prawn paste into one corner of the tray: it is very pungent when it is raw, but turns nutty and savoury once roasted. Roast in the oven for 8 minutes until the ingredients are fragrant and aromatic and starting to caramelise.

4. Remove the tray from the oven, then place the roasted ingredients in a food processor or blender. Purée all the ingredients with the salt and white pepper until smooth. Start with the most fibrous and hard ingredients: purée the lemongrass, ginger and coriander roots first, then add the remaining roasted ingredients. Add 100 ml of water to loosen the paste.

5. To cook the paste, heat the remaining oil in a heavy-based frying pan over medium–high heat. Cook the mixture slowly for about 20 minutes, stirring regularly to avoid sticking. Add the turmeric and kaffir lime leaves and cook for about 20 minutes until aromatic and fragrant. Add the coconut cream and simmer until reduced by half. Add the fish sauce and lime juice and mix through.

6. Divide the paste into 3 portions. It is now ready for other ingredients, such as meat, fish or vegetables to be added to it (see page 156) or to be frozen for future use.

It's important not to add the turmeric to the food processor or blender as it will dye everything yellow! Only add the turmeric when you are cooking the paste.

CHEF'S TIP

Green curry paste

serves 6

• • • • •

preparation
15 minutes

cooking
35 minutes

The paste is the most time-consuming element of making a curry. Make a big batch of any of these delicious curry pastes, then keep them in the refrigerator or freezer in small batches until needed.

fresh

4 cm piece of ginger, peeled and chopped

4 garlic cloves, peeled

4 lemongrass stems, tough outer leaves removed and stems chopped

6 coriander roots, washed and chopped (if you can't get the roots, use double the quantity of stems)

2 small red (Spanish) onions

5 green chillies, seeded and chopped

3 kaffir lime leaves

juice of 1 lime

spices

1 teaspoon ground turmeric

pantry/larder

1 teaspoon salt

1 tablespoon vegetable oil

400 ml coconut cream

1 tablespoon fish sauce

1. Purée the ginger, garlic, lemongrass and coriander roots in a food processor or blender and pulse the ingredients until smooth. Add the salt to help break the ingredients down.

2. Add the onions and chillies and a splash of water and purée to a semismooth paste. In this raw state the paste can be kept in the refrigerator for 3–4 days in an airtight container.

3. Heat the oil in a heavy-based pan over low to medium heat. Add the puréed paste, ground turmeric and kaffir lime leaves and cook, stirring to avoid it sticking, for about 20 minutes until aromatic.

4. Add the coconut cream and gently simmer for about 10 minutes until reduced by about a third.

5. Add the lime juice and fish sauce and stir.

6. Divide the paste into 3 portions. It is now ready for other ingredients, such as meat, fish or vegetables to be added to it (see page 154). At this stage the paste can be kept in the refrigerator for up to 1 week, or frozen for future use.

Geng gari curry paste

fresh

3 cm piece of ginger, peeled

4 red chillies, seeded

3 lemongrass stems, tough outer leaves removed
and stems chopped

6 garlic cloves

3 red onions, chopped

juice of 2 limes

spices

1 teaspoon ground cumin

1 teaspoon ground coriander

1 teaspoon ground cinnamon

1 teaspoon ground nutmeg

1 teaspoon ground turmeric

pantry/larder

1 teaspoon salt

1 tablespoon vegetable oil

660 ml coconut cream

1 tablespoon tamarind pulp

2 tablespoons light soy sauce

1. Purée the ginger, chillies, lemongrass, garlic and salt in a food processor or blender to a smooth paste. Add the onions and purée again. Add a little water to help bring it together to form a smooth paste.

2. Heat the oil in a heavy-based frying pan over medium–high heat for 1 minute. Add the ground spices and cook for about 2 minutes until fragrant. Add the puréed paste and reduce the heat to low and cook slowly for 25–30 minutes, stirring frequently to avoid sticking, until aromatic.

3. Add the coconut cream and simmer for about 5 minutes until reduced by half. The cooked paste at this point can be kept in the refrigerator for 1 week or in the freezer for 3 months.

4. Add the lime juice, tamarind and light soy sauce, then taste to check the balance of flavours and adjust if needed.

5. Divide the paste into 3 portions. It is now ready for other ingredients, such as meat, fish or vegetables to be added to it (see page 166) or to be frozen for future use.

A geng gari curry has a base of spices, such as cinnamon, cumin and coriander, that are fried until aromatic before the rest of the paste is added. This gives a great depth of flavour. It could be used for a vegetarian or meat curry.

serves 4-6

• • • • – • • • • • •

preparation
10 minutes

cooking
35–40 minutes

Hot & sour orange curry paste

fresh

4 lemongrass stems, tough outer leaves removed and stems finely chopped

6 coriander roots, cleaned and finely chopped

4 cm piece of ginger, peeled and finely chopped

5 red chillies, seeded and finely chopped

4 garlic cloves

2 red onions, coarsely chopped

1 red capsicum, coarsely chopped

4 kaffir lime leaves

juice of 3 limes

spices

2 teaspoons ground turmeric

pantry/larder

1 teaspoon salt

1 tablespoon vegetable oil

660 ml coconut cream

3 tablespoons tamarind pulp

2 tablespoons fish sauce

1. Purée the lemongrass, coriander roots, ginger, chillies, garlic and salt in a food processor or blender to a smooth paste, then add the onions and capsicum and purée again. Add a little water to help bring it together to form a smooth paste.

2. Heat the oil in a heavy-based pan over medium–high heat. Add the puréed curry paste and cook the mixture slowly for 20–30 minutes, stirring regularly to avoid sticking. Add the turmeric and kaffir lime leaves and cook the paste for about 30 minutes over low heat until aromatic.

3. When the paste has been cooked, add the coconut cream and simmer for 5 minutes until reduced by half. Add the lime juice, tamarind pulp and fish sauce, then taste to check the balance of flavours and adjust if needed.

4. Divide the paste into 3 portions. It is now ready for other ingredients, such as meat, fish or vegetables to be added to it (see page 160) or to be frozen for future use.

This fantastic Royal Thai curry paste is a vibrant yellow–orange from the turmeric and is often used for a fish curry.

serves 4-6

● ● ● ● — ● ● ● ● ●

preparation
10 minutes

cooking
1 hour

Massaman curry paste
with toasted peanuts

A massaman curry is an amazingly delicious,
fragrant and aromatic curry. It is similar to an
Indian curry and was brought to Thailand by
Muslim and Arab traders from Persia.

serves 8

●●●●●●●

preparation
20 minutes

soaking
30 minutes

cooking
30 minutes

fresh

2 red onions, coarsely chopped

6 garlic cloves, coarsely chopped

5 cm piece of ginger or galangal, peeled and coarsely chopped

4 coriander roots, washed and chopped

3 lemongrass stems, tough outer leaves removed and stems coarsely chopped

spices

3 long dried red chillies

2 teaspoons coriander seeds

1 teaspoon cumin seeds

4 cloves

½ teaspoon ground nutmeg

2 cm cinnamon stick

4 green cardamom pods

3 bay leaves

pantry/larder

100 g blanched skinless peanuts

vegetable oil, for cooking

salt 1–2 tablespoons grated palm sugar

2 tablespoons fish sauce

2 tablespoons tamarind pulp

100 ml pineapple juice

1. Soak the dried chillies in boiling water for about 30 minutes until soft. When soft, remove the seeds and finely chop the flesh.

2. Dry-roast the blanched skinless peanuts until golden brown. Place all the spices in a dry pan and toast for about 3–4 minutes until fragrant and aromatic. Transfer to a mortar and pestle or spice grinder and grind to a medium–fine powder. Sift the ground spices to get rid of any husks and woody bits.

3. Heat 1 tablespoon of vegetable oil in a wok over medium–high heat and fry the chillies, onions, garlic, ginger, coriander roots and lemongrass for about 10 minutes until brown and fragrant. Add a little water if they are starting to catch.

4. Transfer to a food processor or blender and purée with some salt, the sifted spices and the peanuts to a smooth paste.

5. Heat a heavy-based frying pan over medium–high heat. Add a little oil, then cook the smooth paste for about 10 minutes, stirring regularly to avoid sticking, until aromatic. Add a splash of water if it begins to catch or burn.

6. When you can smell the dried spices, add the palm sugar and cook for about 5 minutes until caramelised.

7. Add the fish sauce and tamarind pulp, stir in the pineapple juice and cook for another 5 minutes. Taste to check the balance of flavours and adjust if necessary.

8. Divide the paste into 3 portions. It is now ready for other ingredients, such as meat, fish or vegetables to be added to it (see page 162) or to be frozen for future use.

CHEF'S TIP

This paste can be used for a lamb, beef or chicken curry and can be kept in the freezer for 3 months.

serves 4-6
●●●●–●●●●●

preparation
5 minutes

marinating
1 hour

Spice marinade
for duck or chicken

You can use this marinade on a slow-roasted whole duck (like a Chinese-style roast duck) or chicken, or on duck or chicken breasts cooked quickly on the grill.

fresh
2 garlic cloves, finely chopped
4 cm piece of ginger, peeled and finely grated
4 coriander roots, washed and finely chopped
juice of 1 orange

spices
1 teaspoon ground coriander
1 teaspoon ground cumin
1 teaspoon ground cardamom

pantry/larder
1 tablespoon fish sauce
1 teaspoon palm sugar, grated
1 teaspoon ground black pepper

1. Combine all the ingredients in a bowl to make a marinade.

2. Coat the duck or chicken in the mixture and set aside to marinate for 1 hour before cooking.

6 dressings

The dressings in Thai cooking are what really make the individual dishes sing and mark this cuisine as a tongue-tingling firework display. The balance of taste is very important, so make sure you taste your dressing before you serve it so that it suits your palate.

Thai red chilli vinegar

This is a brilliantly addictive Thai dressing, and is great with grilled or roasted meat, particularly spiced grilled roast beef (see page 94).

serves 4-6

● ● ● ● – ● ● ● ● ●

preparation
5 minutes

fresh

2 long red chillies, seeded and finely chopped

4 cm piece of ginger, peeled and finely grated

1 garlic clove, finely chopped

juice of 1 lime

pantry/larder

¼ teaspoon salt

¼ teaspoon caster sugar

2 tablespoons rice vinegar

1. Put the chillies, ginger and garlic in a mortar and pestle with the salt and sugar and pound to a smooth paste.

2. Add the vinegar and lime juice and mix together. Add 60 ml of water to thin the dressing and add a little extra sugar if necessary. This dressing will keep for 1 week in the refrigerator.

Sang wa dressing

Sang wa is a truly delicious way of curing fish or shellfish. It takes about 4 minutes to cure thin slices of fish (see below) and the result is spectacular.

serves 4-6

• • •• — •• • • •

preparation
10 minutes

marinating
5 minutes

fresh

1 garlic clove

1½ red chillies, seeded and finely chopped

3 tablespoons orange juice

3 tablespoons lime juice

4 cm piece of ginger, peeled and finely grated

1 lemongrass stem, tough outer leaves removed and stem thinly sliced

2 spring onions, thinly sliced

3 kaffir lime leaves, stemmed and thinly sliced

3 coriander sprigs, leaves picked and finely shredded

pantry/larder

½ teaspoon salt

½ teaspoon caster sugar

1. Put the garlic, half the chillies and the salt and sugar in a mortar and pestle and pound to a smooth paste. Add the orange and lime juice and mix to make a marinade.

2. Put the remaining ingredients in a bowl and pour the marinade over. Leave to marinate for 5 minutes before using. This dressing will keep for 2–3 days in the refrigerator.

Variation:

You can use this dressing to cure fish. Put 400 g thinly sliced white fish fillets in a shallow dish. Pour over the dressing and leave for 4–5 minutes to cure and marinate. The acidity will literally cook the fish.

Hot & sour red chilli dressing

This is a classic dipping sauce that is packed full of flavour. Serve with grilled prawns or chicken, as a dipping sauce with oysters or as a salad dressing.

serves 4-6
●●●●–●●●●●

preparation
5 minutes

cooking
2 minutes

fresh

1 garlic clove, finely chopped
2 cm piece of ginger, peeled and finely chopped
2 long red chillies, seeded and finely chopped
juice of 2 limes

pantry/larder

2 teaspoons rice vinegar
1 teaspoon caster sugar
2 tablespoons fish sauce

1. Put 75 ml of water in a saucepan with the vinegar and sugar. Bring to the boil and continue to boil for 1 minute until the sugar has dissolved. Leave it to cool.

2. Mix the garlic, ginger and chilli with the vinegar mixture and add the lime juice and fish sauce. Taste to check the balance of flavours and adjust if needed.

3. This dressing will keep for 2–3 days in the refrigerator.

Chilli tamarind caramel

This is a delicious dressing combining all the elements of Thai cooking. It can be used on grilled fish, prawns, chicken skewers or as a salad dressing.

serves 4
••••

preparation
10 minutes

fresh
4 cm piece of ginger, peeled and finely grated

2 red chillies, seeded and finely chopped

1 garlic clove, finely chopped

juice of 2 limes

pantry/larder
1 tablespoon vegetable oil

50 g palm sugar, grated (or soft brown sugar)

1 tablespoon honey

50 g tamarind pulp

2 tablespoons fish sauce

1. Heat a splash of oil in a frying pan over medium heat. Fry the ginger, chillies and garlic for about 2 minutes until fragrant and aromatic. Add the palm sugar and honey and cook for 3–4 minutes to slowly caramelise.

2. When golden brown, add the tamarind pulp, fish sauce and 80 ml of water and simmer for about 5 minutes until sticky and caramelised.

3. Remove the pan from the heat and add the lime juice. Taste to check the balance of flavours and adjust if needed: it should be hot from the chilli and ginger, sweet from the palm sugar and honey, sour from the tamarind and lime juice and salty from the fish sauce.

4. This dressing will keep for about 1 week in the refrigerator.

Red chilli nahm jim dressing

serves 4-6
● ● ●● – ● ● ● ● ●

preparation
10 minutes

fresh
2 garlic cloves
3 red chillies, seeded and finely chopped
3 coriander roots, washed and chopped
juice of 3 limes

pantry/larder
½ teaspoon salt
1 teaspoon grated palm sugar
3 tablespoons fish sauce

1. Put the garlic, chillies and coriander roots in a mortar and pestle with the salt and sugar and pound to a smooth paste. Add the lime juice and fish sauce.

2. Taste the dressing to check the balance of flavours and adjust if needed: the sauce should be hot from the chilli, sweet from the orange and sugar, refreshingly acidic with the lime juice and salty from the fish sauce.

3. This dressing will keep for about 4–6 days in the refrigerator.

Green chilli nahm jim dressing

serves 4-6

• • •• — •• • • •

preparation
10 minutes

fresh
2 garlic cloves
3 coriander roots, washed and chopped
4 long green chillies, seeded and finely chopped
3 coriander sprigs, leaves picked
juice of 3 limes

pantry/larder
1 teaspoon salt
1 teaspoon caster sugar
2 tablespoons fish sauce

1. Put the garlic and coriander roots in a mortar and pestle and pound to a smooth paste. Add the green chillies, salt and sugar and pound again. Add the coriander leaves and continue to pound to a bright green paste.

2. Add the lime juice and fish sauce. Add 50 ml of water to loosen the paste and dilute the acidity.

3. This dressing will keep for about 4–5 days in the refrigerator.

CHEF'S TIP
Serve grilled or spice-roasted meat with the dressing splashed over the top or as a dipping sauce.

3 chillies

Chilli releases endorphins and is addictive, so the more you eat, the better you feel and the more you crave. A good sweet chilli sauce should have a balance of hot, sweet, salt and sour. You could make a large quantity, put it in sterilised jars and give them as gifts at Christmas. Chilli jams or relishes are the perfect partner to many Thai dishes.

Sweet chilli sauce

serves 4-6

• • •• – • • • • •

preparation
10 minutes

cooking
12 minutes

fresh
200 g red chillies, seeded
4 cm piece of ginger, peeled and finely grated
4 garlic cloves

pantry/larder
200 g caster sugar
1 tablespoon salt
100 g rice vinegar

1. Put the red chillies, ginger and garlic in a food processor or blender and blitz to a chunky paste.

2. Put the sugar, salt, vinegar and 100 ml of water in a large heavy-based saucepan and bring to the boil. Add the blended mixture and simmer for another 10 minutes.

3. Remove from the heat and set aside to cool. Pour into a sterilised jar and store for up to 2–3 weeks in the refrigerator.

Fresh chilli jam

serves 4-6

● ● ●● – ● ● ● ● ●

preparation
10 minutes

cooking
25 minutes

fresh

two 4 cm pieces of ginger, peeled and finely grated

12 long red chillies, seeded and finely chopped

6 garlic cloves, peeled and chopped

6 coriander roots and stems, washed and finely chopped

16 roma tomatoes

1 brown onion, finely chopped

juice of 2 limes

spices

freshly ground black pepper

pantry/larder

200 g soft brown sugar

3 tablespoons fish sauce

2 tablespoons tamarind pulp

salt

1. Put the ginger, chillies, garlic and coriander roots and stems in a food processor or blender and pulse to a rough paste. Add half the tomatoes and the onion and pulse to a purée.

2. Transfer the purée to a saucepan and add the sugar, fish sauce and tamarind. Cook over medium heat for about 25 minutes until the purée starts to be syrupy and the liquid has reduced.

3. Cut the remaining tomatoes in half and remove the seeds. Finely chop the flesh and add to the pan. Season well with salt and black pepper and add the lime juice. Taste to check the balance of flavours and adjust if necessary, then remove from the heat. As it cools, it will condense to a syrupy paste.

4. This jam will keep for about 10–14 days in the refrigerator; however, I doubt that it will last that long as you will have eaten it before you need to worry about a use-by date.

CHEF'S TIP

Serve with just about anything, from scrambled eggs to grilled chicken, or use as a base for a dressing.

Nam prik pow Thai chilli relish

serves 4-6
●●●●–●●●●●

preparation
15 minutes

cooking
1 hour

There are many different versions for chilli (prik) relishes, pastes and jams where the ingredients are either roasted or fried separately or cooked in a pan together to form these delicious condiments.

fresh

4 large red chillies, seeded and finely chopped

4 garlic cloves, chopped

4 cm piece of ginger, peeled and chopped

3 onions, coarsely chopped

juice of 2 limes

spices

¼ teaspoon crushed dried red chillies

2 teaspoons ground cinnamon

1 teaspoon ground coriander

pantry/larder

3 tablespoons vegetable oil

2 tablespoons soft brown sugar

½ teaspoon salt

3 tablespoons tamarind pulp

2 tablespoons fish sauce

1. Preheat the oven to 200°C.

2. Put the chilli, garlic, ginger and onions in a bowl with half the oil and mix together. Spread this mixture out on a roasting tray, then roast in the oven for 20 minutes until the onion and garlic are soft and starting to caramelise.

3. Transfer to a food processor or blender and add the brown sugar, salt and spices and blend to a paste. Add the tamarind, fish sauce and 100 ml water and continue to blend to a smooth pulp.

4. Heat the remaining oil in a heavy-based saucepan over medium–high heat. Transfer the puréed mixture to the pan, lower the heat and cook for 40 minutes until the excess liquid has cooked away and the paste is turning to a jam-like consistency.

5. Add the lime juice and mix together. Taste to check the balance of flavours and adjust if needed. Pour into sterilised jars and store in the refrigerator for up to 1 month.

CHEF'S TIP Make a large batch, then store in sterilised jars like a jam or chutney so that you can use it for anything from a beef stir-fry to a cooked breakfast or to transform a sandwich.

serves 4-6
●●●●–●●●●●

preparation
10 minutes

cooking
10 minutes

Peanut dipping sauce

This is a delicious dipping sauce with lots of great taste and texture. You could serve it with any roasted or grilled meat, but it is especially good with the Salt and spice-roast pork belly (see page 100).

fresh

3 coriander roots, washed and finely chopped

1 garlic clove, finely chopped

1 red chilli, seeded and finely chopped

4 shallots, finely chopped

juice of 1 lime

2 coriander sprigs, leaves picked and chopped

spices

freshly ground black pepper

pantry/larder

salt

2 tablespoons light vegetable oil

2 teaspoons grated palm sugar

4 tablespoons blanched skinless peanuts, toasted

1 tablespoon light soy sauce

1. Put the coriander roots and garlic in a mortar and pestle and pound with a pinch of salt until smooth. Add the red chilli and shallots and continue to pound to a smooth paste.

2. Heat a heavy-based pan over medium–high heat. Add half the oil and the spice paste and fry for about 2 minutes until fragrant. Add the palm sugar and cook for 4 minutes until caramelised.

3. Add the toasted peanuts and continue to cook for 3–4 minutes until the peanuts are a deep golden brown. If the sugar begins to scorch, add a splash of water.

4. Remove the mixture from the pan, return it to the mortar and pestle and pound to a semismooth paste.

5. Stir in the remaining oil, soy sauce and lime juice. Add about 60 ml of water to thin the sauce and add the coriander. Serve with crispy pork or chicken satay.

6. This sauce will keep for about 1 week in the refrigerator.

Relishes & pickles

Relishes and pickles are great with grilled or roasted meat such as the Slow roast pork shoulder (see page 104) or the Sweet and crispy pork spare ribs (see page 110). They can accompany roast meat such as chicken, grilled pork or roast duck and would also work well with cooked prawns.

Fresh mango relish

serves 4-6

• • •• – •• • • •

preparation
5 minutes

cooking
12 minutes

fresh

2 ripe mangoes, peeled, stoned and finely chopped
2 green chillies, seeded and finely chopped
juice of 1 lime

spices
½ teaspoon ground cumin
freshly ground black pepper

pantry/larder
salt
1 tablespoon soft brown sugar
2 tablespoons tamarind pulp

1. Mix all of the ingredients, except the lime juice, with 100 ml of water in a small saucepan. Bring to the boil, then lower the heat and simmer for 10 minutes or until the excess water has evaporated.

2. Remove from the heat and leave to cool. Add the lime juice.

3. This relish will keep for 2–3 days in the refrigerator.

Fresh pickle

serves 4-6

• • •• – •• • • •

preparation
10 minutes

fresh

1 medium-hard pear (not too ripe), quartered, cored
and cut into 1 cm cubes

1 hard (unripe) mango, peeled, stoned and cut into
1 cm cubes

1 crisp apple (such as a pink lady or braeburn),
quartered, cored and cut into 1 cm cubes

juice of 1 lime

2 medium–hot red chillies, seeded and finely
chopped

1 small onion, finely diced

3 cm piece of ginger, peeled and finely grated

spices

freshly ground black pepper

pantry/larder

2 tablespoons rice vinegar

1 tablespoon grated palm sugar

salt

1. Mix all of the ingredients together in a bowl
and season well with salt and black pepper. Set
aside to stand for 5 minutes, then taste to check
the balance of flavours and adjust if needed.

2. This pickle will only keep for a couple of
days in the refrigerator: longer than that and the
fruit will become too soft and start to ferment.

Salt & pepper mix

serves 4-6

•••—••••

preparation
10 minutes

cooking
3 minutes

This is a delicious and fragrant dry spice mix that can be used for just about anything: chicken, fish or shellfish are particularly good.

spices

1 tablespoon coriander seeds
2 teaspoons cumin seeds
2 teaspoons fennel seeds
5 whole star anise
½ teaspoon white peppercorns
½ teaspoon black peppercorns
1 teaspoon ground turmeric
pinch of crushed dried chillies

pantry/larder

3 tablespoons coarse salt flakes

1. Put all of the ingredients, except the salt, in a dry frying pan over medium heat and dry-fry for 2–3 minutes until fragrant and aromatic, keeping the spices moving in the pan so that they do not scorch.

2. Transfer to a spice grinder or mortar and pestle and grind to a medium–fine powder: it is good if there is a little texture but you do not want big chunks of spices. Add the salt flakes.

3. This dry spice rub will keep well in an airtight container for a few weeks. Dry-roast the mixture in a frying pan over medium–high heat to refresh the aromatic mixture before using.

CHEF'S TIP
Use to season meat, fish, shellfish or steamed vegetables.

Thai sticky rice

serves 4-6

•••••–••••••

soaking
3 hours

steaming
30 minutes

This is broad short-grained rice that becomes thick and glutinous when it is cooked. Use this rice for the classic Thai sticky rice with mango (see page 204) and other fruit desserts.

fresh

250 g uncooked Thai sticky rice (available from Asian grocery stores)

1. Soak the uncooked rice in water for 3 hours, then drain and rinse thoroughly as it will be very starchy.

2. Set a steamer over a saucepan of water and lay a double layer of muslin or cheesecloth in the steamer. Tip the soaked rice on top.

3. Steam the rice over medium heat for 30 minutes until sticky and glutinous.

This rice must be manually steamed: it does not work well in an electric steamer.

Menu planner

When you eat Thai food, you do not have just one dish, instead you have a series of dishes that complement and contrast with each other. When planning a menu you have to think of the meal as a whole: what was eaten before and what will follow are important. There should be a balance of peppery hot, sweet, saltiness and sour. This balance of taste should be present in every dish and across the whole meal. Some dishes are mild and others spicy. Some dishes are smooth while others have more texture. One dish may be hot and salty while the next one is hot and sour. Colour, taste and texture are all important.

When preparing the ingredients, look at all the recipes for your meal and write a prep list. There may be ginger in a few of the dishes so chop it once, then divide the ginger for each dish. Lay out your prepped ingredients on a plate or tray like an artist's palette: grated ginger, next to chopped spring onions, next to chilli or garlic. If you follow this method, it is then easy to think about a meal with four or five components.

SATURDAY LUNCH : Tamarind fried prawns (see page 38), Barbecued pork & herb salad (see page 92), Hot & sour orange curry with grilled salmon (see page 160), Toasted coconut ice-cream topping (see page 212), Pineapple, lime & mint crush (see page 216)

SIMPLE DINNER : Thai beef skewers with red chilli vinegar (see page 88), Grilled prawn & basil salad (see page 62), Coconut & roast chicken soup (see page 172), Pineapple with caramelised chilli sauce (see page 208), Watermelon with lime, salt & black pepper (see page 210)

FRIENDS COMING OVER : Crispy chicken spring rolls (see page 28), Crab & lime salad (see page 74), Slow-roasted pork shoulder with coriander, tamarind & chilli (see page 104), Stir-fried spinach (see page 194), Mango & pineapple salad (see page 206)

WANT TO IMPRESS : Kung sang wa cured prawns (see page 36), Roast duck salad with mango & toasted coconut (see page 78), Turmeric grilled fish (see page 130), Thai green curry with prawns (see page 154), Banana & coconut pancakes (see page 214)

MIDWEEK DINNER : Grilled squid with garlic & pepper (see page 40), Pork & pickled cucumber salad (see page 72), Sesame-seared tuna with lemongrass & ginger (see page 124), Pad thai fried noodles (see page 176), Toasted coconut ice-cream topping (see page 212)

MIDWEEK DINNER : Chicken satay (see page 32), Crisp cabbage & coriander salad (see page 66), Crispy fried whitebait with Thai spices (see page 126), Salt & spice-roast pork belly (see page 100), Sticky rice with mango (see page 204)

SOMETHING SPECIAL : Fried crab cakes with coriander (see page 50), Sesame chicken salad with white pepper (see page 64), Coconut fish curry (see page 152), Spicy beef noodles with kaffir lime leaves (see page 180), Roasted fruits with aromatic Thai spices (see page 218)

Index

Acknowledgments

From Tom Kime

I would like to thank all the chefs and food lovers who have inspired me over many years. This book is for you.

Thank you to both Katie Newton John and Maureen Miller for their generosity and patience having the team invade their beautiful homes and allowing us to shoot there.

I would like to thank Lisa Linder for her amazing photographs and Aya Nishimura and Ross Dobson for making my food look so delicious. A huge thank you to Catie Ziller, Abi Waters and Alice Chadwick for bringing this great project to life.

Thank you to my wife, Kylie, for her tireless support and all the great things we share. I love you.

Thank you to my boys, Alexander and Orlando, for being such enthusiastic eaters and making mealtimes such a highlight of our day.

To my sister Hannah, for being so courageous. I hope you enjoy using this book, I thought of you when I was writing it.

Thank you to my dad Robert, for teaching me how to look at things and appreciate what is good.

To my mum Helen, who gave her love to people through her amazing food and taught me the love of cooking.

Thank you.

From Lisa Linder

A big thank you to Tammy, Jim and Rebecca for kindly putting us up and helping us enormously throughout the shoot. And Amelia Wasiliev for driving miles with her gorgeous props, always with a big smile :-).

And the lovely Chaz for giving up her time and modelling for us so beautifully.

TOM KIME has worked in some of the best restaurants in London and Sydney. He has travelled extensively to discover and sample the world's best street food. Having cut his catering teeth with Rick Stein, Tom has worked at the River Café alongside Jamie Oliver (he cooked at Jamie's wedding) and at Darley Street Thai with David Thompson. His first book, *Exploring Taste and Flavour*, published in 2005 (now retitled *Tasting*), won a World Gourmand Award. The 2007 World Gourmand Awards presented a silver medal to his second book, *Street Food*. In 2015 *Fish Tales*, Tom's fifth book, was honoured by the World Gourmand Awards as one of their Best of the Best books from the last 20 years. Tom has also presented three of his own television series and filmed five series of the popular Australian series *Ready Steady Cook*. More recently, Tom is the Group Executive Head Chef of GoodTime hospitality in Sydney and was the Executive Chef at Fish & Co., the sustainable seafood café in Sydney from 2010–2015. He works as an international food consultant, writer and presenter.

- -

Published in 2017 by Murdoch Books, an imprint of Allen & Unwin.
First published by Hachette Livre (Marabout) in 2017.

Murdoch Books Australia
83 Alexander Street
Crows Nest NSW 2065
Phone: +61 (0) 2 8425 0100
Fax: +61 (0) 2 9906 2218
murdochbooks.com.au
info@murdochbooks.com.au

Murdoch Books UK
Ormond House
26–27 Boswell Street
London WC1N 3JZ
Phone: +44 (0) 20 8785 5995
murdochbooks.co.uk
info@murdochbooks.co.uk

For Corporate Orders & Custom Publishing, contact our Business Development Team at salesenquiries@murdochbooks.com.au.

Publisher: Corinne Roberts
Editor: Melody Lord
Photographer: Lisa Linder
Illustrations: Alice Chadwick
Food and prop stylist: Aya Nishimura
Home economist: Ross Dobson
Production: Lou Playfair

© Hachette Livre (Marabout) 2017

A cataloguing-in-publication entry is available from the catalogue of the National Library of Australia at nla.gov.au.

ISBN 978 1 76052 274 2 Australia
ISBN 978 1 76052 776 1 UK

A catalogue record for this book is available from the British Library.

Printed by C & C Offset Printing Co. Ltd., China